THE GOLD MINE EFFECT

Rasmus Ankersen

THE GOLD MINE EFFECT

CRACK THE SECRETS OF HIGH PERFORMANCE

ICON

Published in the UK in 2012 by
Icon Books Ltd, Omnibus Business Centre,
39–41 North Road, London N7 9DP
email: info@iconbooks.co.uk
www.iconbooks.co.uk

Sold in the UK, Europe, South Africa and Asia
by Faber & Faber Ltd, Bloomsbury House,
74–77 Great Russell Street,
London WC1B 3DA or their agents

Distributed in the UK, Europe, South Africa and Asia
by TBS Ltd, TBS Distribution Centre, Colchester Road,
Frating Green, Colchester CO7 7DW

Published in Australia in 2012 by Allen & Unwin Pty Ltd,
PO Box 8500, 83 Alexander Street,
Crows Nest, NSW 2065

Distributed in Canada by Penguin Books Canada,
90 Eglinton Avenue East, Suite 700,
Toronto, Ontario M4P 2YE

ISBN: 978-184831-399-6

Typeset in ITC Galliard by Marie Doherty

Printed and bound in the UK
by CPI Group (UK) Ltd, Croydon, CR0 4YY

Contents

About the author

Rasmus Ankersen is a bestselling author, a motivational speaker on performance development and a trusted advisor to businesses and athletes around the world. He wrote his first book *The DNA of a Winner* at the age of 22. A year later he published his second, *Leader DNA*, based on field studies of 25 high-profile leaders, including the Secretary of NATO, Anders Fogh Rasmussen, and the CEO of LEGO Group, Jorgen Vig Knudstorp. *Leader DNA* has been the best-selling leadership book in Denmark for the last five years. In his home country Rasmus has also won a Berlingske Business Magazine award, being named one of the three biggest business talents in Denmark, and the Danish prime minister recently invited him to contribute a chapter to his new book *The Danish Dream*.

With *The Gold Mine Effect* Rasmus has taken another step into the secrets of high performance, becoming the only expert on the subject who has literally lived and trained with the best athletes on the planet. Now back in London, Rasmus is teaching organisations how to build their own Gold Mines of world-class performance, through real-life examples and result-driven insights.

You can find out more about Rasmus at www.rasmusankersen.com.

Henrik Hyldgaard is the co-author of *The Gold Mine Effect* and has been working as Rasmus's personal sparring partner for the last three years. Henrik is a brand strategist and master of business creativity. In late 2012 he will be publishing his book *Hotel Creativity – Check in and Change the Destiny of Your Company*. Check him out at www.hotelcreativity.com.

Acknowledgements

Expeditions are rarely the kind of thing you can manage on your own, and creating this book has certainly not been a one-man show. I would like to thank all those who have helped me along the way – any over-simplifications or mistakes are my responsibility, and mine alone.

I would like first and foremost to offer my sincere thanks to all the athletes, coaches and parents in the six Gold Mines. They opened their doors to me, allowing me to become part of their daily lives and to follow them closely.

I would also like to thank all the people who established contacts for me along the way and who moved some of the obstacles in my path, opening my way to the hearts of the Gold Mines.

Not least, I would like to offer the enormous thanks to my co-author Henrik Hyldgaard for his indispensable efforts and world-class sparring. Without his invaluable advice the book would never have become what it is.

Finally, the biggest thank yous of all go to my mother Joan and father Søren for giving me the roots to grow, the wings to fly and the freedom to make mistakes.

The Simon Kjaer problem

I shall start with an admission: if everything in my life had gone as I hoped and believed it would, this book would never have been written.

I spent my boyhood in rural western Denmark, in a little town in the middle of nowhere. It had a population of 35,000 and its only claim to fame was as a hotspot of the Danish textile industry.

With the focus of that industry rapidly moving away to Eastern Europe and China, there seemed little sense in dreaming of a future as a textile magnate. Instead, I fantasised about being a footballer and playing on famous pitches across the world. The walls of my room were covered in posters of great players. After school every day I played on the street with the other boys in the neighbourhood. I even promised my dad I would buy him a Mercedes once my professional career took off. And at the age of eighteen I was made captain of one of Denmark's best youth teams. Life was good.

But just one year later, my dream was over. I smashed up my knee so badly in my first league match at the age of nineteen that I would never be able to play professionally again. A promising career ended before it had even begun.

I have to admit that as a footballer I am now nothing but an injured-then-forgotten has-been. Like many other injured and forgotten players, I ended up working as a coach. The best coaches are often frustrated players with pent-up ambitions.

In 2004 I helped establish Scandinavia's first football academy. In those days we didn't have much more than a couple of grass pitches with cows grazing on the other side of the fence and a primitive building where we could put the players up for the night. Our ambition of creating world-class players at this desolate location in western Denmark must have seemed naive. I still remember how we had to struggle to attract players for the academy's first intake. As newcomers to the business we were unable to entice those players considered to be the most talented in the country – we simply had to take what we could get. It was rather reminiscent of the way kids pick their teams at school. We were the last to pick and had to take what was left over when the other clubs had made their choices.

Eventually we had signed contracts with fifteen or sixteen boys and were only short of one player. One of the candidates was a fifteen-year-old boy from a town 50 kilometres from the academy. His name was Simon Kjaer. He belonged to the anonymous majority the Danish club scouts had no record of in their archives. In fact, we had already decided that we didn't want him. Several of the academy's coaches had seen him play, myself included, and all were agreed: 'He hasn't made a mark and he never will.'

But the season was about to start. We didn't have much time, and we didn't really have any other options, so we decided to give Simon Kjaer the last place anyway. He was the quickest solution, and his father had a job as materials manager at the club (read: he was good at his job and we were willing to go a long way to keep him). Simon Kjaer was accepted on the condition that he paid for his own keep. As Simon remembers it himself: 'My impression was that they only accepted me because they couldn't hire players who were better than me. The best of them had turned the opportunity down.'

He was absolutely right.

The big mistake

Flash forward seven years. I am sitting in the stands at the Olympic Stadium in Rome watching an Italian Serie A match between Roma and Juventus. The match is not only special because it is between two of Europe's very best clubs, but also because it is the debut of Roma's new 22-year-old centre back.

It is this blond-haired Dane I have my eye on from my seat among the euphoric Roma fans. As he jogs about clapping at the crowd, I think back to the first time I met him. It was at FC Midtjylland's football academy in Denmark, where I was coach.

Things have moved fast since then for Simon Kjaer.

He was first sold to Palermo in Italy for £3.3 million when he was just eighteen years old. At twenty he was sold on to Wolfsburg in Germany for £9.2 million. And now, still in his early twenties, he is with Roma – a major club. Playing in a position that most players only master in their late twenties or early thirties, he has rapidly become one of the stand-out players in the Italian league, a league which historically has produced some of the world's best defenders. Every weekend he is matched against enormously accomplished strikers, and his first season in the Serie A has culminated in his selection for the team of the year alongside players such as the legendary Paolo Maldini. Experts have called him one of the world's most promising defenders, and major clubs like Manchester United, AC Milan and Liverpool have been down on their knees begging to sign him, and still are.

The big shock

According to conventional wisdom, Simon Kjaer's success should be the story of a boy born with an extraordinary innate talent coming in to his own. This is certainly the explanation coaches, journalists and experts resort to when trying to explain his performance. They are, however, mistaken. His story is of anything but raw, inbred talent.

I still remember the day back in 2004 when Claus Stenlein, the director of the FC Midtjylland Football Academy, came into the coaches' office with a pile of paper slips in his hand. It was just six months after Simon Kjaer had joined the academy. All the coaches were present in the room, myself included. Claus dealt out the slips and asked us each to write down the names of the five players we thought would go furthest in five years, in order of priority. At that time we had sixteen players to choose from. One of them was Simon Kjaer. When we had all written five names, the academy director sealed them into an envelope and put them away in a drawer.

Five years later, just after Kjaer was sold for £3.3 million, Claus Steinlein reopened the envelope. Out of eight coaches, how many do you think had Simon Kjaer's name on their list?

Not one of us!

World War Three

You have to understand that none of the eight coaches that rejected Simon were amateurs. On the contrary; we were intelligent, highly trained, and we all had a UEFA A-license. Although between us we had more than a hundred years of experience in talent development, each and every one of us well and truly screwed up. How could we have been so mistaken? What exactly did we overlook? I have been asking myself that question every day since.

The case of Simon Kjaer is more responsible for the birth of this book than any other experience I have had and, as you will realise the more you read, his story is by no means unique. Coaches, managers, parents and teachers, in any field whatsoever, all have to deal with their own Simon Kjaer problem. He confronts us all with numerous questions, which need to be addressed regardless of what industry you work in or where in the world you find yourself. What is talent? Do we actually know what the word means? Do we even know what we are looking for? How can we identify talent? How is it grown? And how can we grow it more effectively?

The answers to these questions are more valuable now than ever before. Talent is an absolutely crucial factor in the economic struggles taking place in the 21st century. Success or failure for both organisations and nations in the global marketplace is decided by their TQ (talent quotient) – the ability to capitalise on the talent they have at their disposal. A new world war is already breaking out, one that will be fought not with weapons but with talent. Anyone who does not take this challenge seriously will be crushed in the global competition. According to calculations by the World Economic Forum, for example, Europe and the United States, usually number one on the Global Talent Index, will not be in a position to maintain their levels of prosperity unless they develop their workforces with 72 million more qualified workers before 2030. As Anna Janczak, the World Economic Forum director says: 'No-one will escape unscathed. Everyone will be confronted with the global lack of talent over the years to come.'

Aggressive talent strategies

It may seem like a luxury for Western nations to prioritise talent development in these times of crisis when they are suffering from low growth and stagnating productivity. But talent development may prove to be one of our most important tools with which to dig our way out of the economic crisis, not least in the light of the fact that rapidly growing, ambitious countries like China, South Korea and Singapore have all launched national talent strategies – recognition of the fact that their TQ is one of their greatest assets. Although these nations are already enjoying high growth rates, they are obviously aware of the fact that without constant and effective capitalisation of their talent mass they will not be able to maintain their current rate of progress.

The Chinese government, for example, has launched what is probably the most comprehensive national talent strategy, with a ten-year action plan. According to President

Hu Jintao, who spearheaded the strategy himself, over the next ten years China must transform its current labour-intensive economy to a strong talent-based economy. This means, among other things, that by 2020, 15 per cent of the country's GDP must be invested in education and research. The number of scientists must be increased to 3.8 million. By way of comparison, the 27 EU countries presently have 1.4 million scientists at their disposal. The Chinese plan includes numerous other initiatives, such as spreading the talent mass by motivating more well-educated people to migrate to poor rural areas, and boosting the recruitment of top management talent for the country's many state-owned enterprises.

Talent development in Singapore is even more aggressive. The country's talent strategy, which goes under the name 'Managed by Elites', is intended to identify and attract the greatest talent in the world to Singapore over the next few years. The country has already allied itself with a number of the world's best universities in order to attract foreign scientists and students by means of lucrative tax schemes and the offer of free education if they stay in Singapore for at least three years. The declared goal is to attract 150,000 top foreign students in 2015. Several teams of talent scouts have already been set up in neighbouring countries to monitor primary and secondary schools, youth training schemes and universities in order to spot the best brains and entice them over to Singapore.

Meanwhile, companies in Brazil have recognised that losing talent overseas is a real problem, and have organised massive campaigns to attract talented citizens back home from the US and Europe.

Even if you cannot keep all your talent at home, you

can exploit the fact that it is spread across the global labour market. India, for example, is currently trying to establish close contact with some of the 25 million Indians who live elsewhere in the world. The goal is to gain access to the knowledge of the nation's 'foreign stars' and make use of their business contacts, expertise and networks to create growth back in India.

Everyone has their own 'Simon Kjaer problem'

On a slightly smaller scale, individual forward-looking businesses are working intensively to develop their TQ. They have realised that without talent, organisations cannot prosper. As the American business author George Anders has pointed out, this is the reason that 208,000 full-time recruiters are working in the United States today, everywhere from General Electric to a three-person firm that specialises in pulp mill operators. Big companies like AT&T, Pfizer and Deloitte now even have 'chief talent officers'. Recently, IT giant Cisco established a talent centre in India with the ambition of sextupling its recruitment of Indian engineers over a period of just five years.

Nobody can afford to lose the global talent war, which these examples demonstrate has already broken out. Every company and every nation has its own Simon Kjaer problem to grapple with and my purpose in this book is to present some specific ideas as to how people in the worlds of business, sport, education and beyond can take concrete steps to improve their TQ.

Having witnessed the remarkable story of Simon Kjaer unfold, it became a personal obsession to crack the TQ code. I decided to quit my job, and used all the money I had left to book six plane tickets. In the seven months that followed, I travelled round the world to live and train in six 'Gold Mines' – small, geographically defined locations which are pumping out top performers assembly-line fashion.

These Gold Mines are:

- Bekoji, a village in Ethiopia where the world's best middle-distance runners are raised.
- South Korea, which produces 35 per cent of the world's best female golfers.
- Kingston, Jamaica, where a single athletics club has succeeded in producing most of the world's best sprinters.
- Russia, which in a matter of a few years has evolved from a nation with an unremarkable tennis reputation to one which has produced 25 per cent of players on the world women's top 40 ranking list.
- Iten, a village in Kenya which consistently produces the world's best long-distance runners.
- Brazil, where a vastly disproportionate number of the world's top football players originate from.

It is these six Gold Mines, and the remarkable people I discovered at each, that you will encounter in this book. Permit me to be your guide on a round-the-world trip to solve the mystery of what lies behind world-class performance.

My hunt for answers started early one morning on a dirt track in Kenya.

The eight Gold Mine concepts

It is 5.30 in the morning and I am standing in the half-light, waiting at the intersection of two red dirt paths. It is here that I have arranged to meet a very special group of people. As I watch, a silhouetted figure appears a bit further up the path, approaching with long, effortless strides. Ten metres away from me, the figure slows down. Christopher Cheboiboch, holder of the fourth fastest time ever in the New York Marathon, is out on his first training run of the day. He stops right in front of me and says hello.

I tell him that I am here to find the secret behind the success of Kenyan runners, and that I am waiting for the training group I have been allowed to follow for the day. He eyes me sceptically, then says, 'People come here from all over the world, convinced that they will be able to suss out the secret behind our runners by lumbering about in the hills with their heart rate monitors, and staying at the four star hotel with a view. But they're looking in entirely the wrong place.'

'Where should they be looking, then?' I ask.

For a few seconds the air between us is perfectly still. Christopher looks down at the red dirt beneath our feet. 'There's only one way to understand the code. Be a Kenyan, live like a Kenyan,' he says. His glance lingers on me for a moment, before he turns about face and disappears off into the gloom once more.

Alone again on this path 2,800 metres above sea level, I try to imagine what it means to be a Kenyan. I start doing exercises to keep my body warm in the wind. Although I can still feel the aftermath of the long flight in my limbs, it does feel wonderful to be here at last.

It isn't long before I hear a low thumping through the red earth, which gradually grows louder and louder. Then, down the hill behind me comes my training group: twelve Kenyan men and boys running at full tilt on, their track-suits slapping audibly in the wind as they head straight towards me.

As they pass I fall in with them, bringing up the rear. Very soon my heart starts to pound. My legs struggle to keep pace even with the rear guard. My fellow runners were

The author running with the Kenyans

all born and bred here in the Rift Valley and are members of the Kalenjin tribe which, numbering three million, constitutes almost 10 per cent of Kenya's population. On these unprepossessing dirt tracks, an incomprehensibly large proportion of the world's best long-distance runners are produced, with the apparent efficiency and predictability of a factory production line.

It is a well-known fact that Kenyans occupy the throne of world long-distance running, but it is less well known that more than 70 per cent of all Kenya's gold medals at international championships have been brought home by Kalenjin athletes. Since 1968, for instance, only one non-Kalenjin runner has succeeded in taking gold in the Olympic steeplechase.

These incredible statistics are the reason that I endeavour to keep pace with the group on this morning in Iten. The morning sun has now awoken and its first rays are falling on the pack that I am a part of as it pushes its way over the top of the hill. It's hard going; my pulse is thumping and my tongue is hanging out of my mouth.

I'm here searching for the answer to one question: how can it be that a single tribe has won such a huge number of gold medals and toppled a succession of long-distance world records?

Closer scrutiny reveals that the mystery of the Kalenjin tribe is not unique. In five other places in the world we find a similar phenomenon – places which produce results that seem inexplicable at first sight.

How did one athletics club, which trains on a diesel-scorched grass track in Kingston, Jamaica, manage to win nine sprint medals at the 2008 Beijing Olympics (five of them gold), one a world record and an Olympic record?

Why do 35 of the world's 100 best women golfers come from South Korea which, with its inhospitably cold climate and astronomical green fees, scares off the vast majority of golfers?

How did it happen than one Ethiopian village in the middle of nowhere won four gold medals in middle-distance running at the latest Olympics?

How can it be that in just a few years Russia has developed from a mediocre tennis nation into one that occupies 25 per cent of the world women's top 40 ranking list?

Why is it that every other year since 1993 a Brazilian has been named the world's best footballer? And how can it be that in 2010, 67 Brazilians played in the world's premier championship, the Champions League, compared to only 25 Britains and 26 Germans, even though not one Brazilian club participated?

Like the Kalenjin tribe, these other Gold Mines of elite performance leave us with a multitude of unanswered questions. With their outstanding results, they challenge our most ingrained convictions as to how elite athletes are created, and they confront us with mysteries that have preoccupied people for generations. What is talent? Why are some people so successful while others fail so miserably? Is there a code we can crack in order to unlock the secret of outstanding performance? If answers to these questions can be found then their application will reach far beyond the world of sport – into the boardrooms, classrooms and homes of the world.

Scientists, journalists and coaches are trying to come up with such answers all the time. The problem is that their ideas are based on observations they have made at a physical distance from the Gold Mines. They therefore present conclusions characterised by oversimplification and rigidity, and unfortunately it's often on the basis of these oversimplifications that coaches, talent scouts, athletes and parents pursue high performance. If we really want to understand why the Gold Mines are such crucibles of talent it is hardly satisfactory to study them from afar. That's why I decided to travel the world to find the answers I was looking for – talking, studying, eating, training and living with people in these places which have apparently cracked the code of high performance.

Over a period of seven months I visited the six Gold Mines to feel for myself what it means to grow up in a Brazilian favela (shanty town) with the dream of becoming one of the world's best footballers; to understand how much is actually at stake for a young runner in the Kenyan Rift Valley; to find out what it takes to make a world-class sprinter in Jamaica; and to learn how Russian and South Korean parents push their children to the limit so that they make it as elite professional tennis players and golfers.

This book presents my findings regarding the ingredients needed to create a Gold Mine, and shows how anyone can use this information to create their own Gold Mine of world-class performance.

Perhaps you're sitting there right now wondering how you can put the ideas and principles behind the Gold Mines to good use if you are not involved in sport? Well, take a moment to read this list. A top performer:

- Must perform under conditions of intense pressure
- Must understand that numbers drive everything
- Is constantly under pressure from ambitious new competitors from all over the world

- Realises that last year's record becomes next year's baseline
- Constantly grows and reinvents themselves in order to stay at the top
- Is subject to brutal accountability: you win or you lose – nothing in between
- Must have sustainable drive, or achieving performance goals becomes difficult.

My guess is that these prerequisites and requirements are almost identical to those you have to perform under in your own industry, whatever it is. At heart, the Gold Mines are about far more than just golf, running or football. They are about the underlying mechanisms which orchestrate world-class performance, and regardless of whether we work in sport, the arts, business or science, we have to understand that all journeys towards realising potential have a great deal more in common than we might first imagine.

The general debate on talent development is full of mis-understandings, clichés, romanticised conceptions, guess-work and outdated knowledge. My aim in this book is to deliver a fresh, highly practical perspective on the subject. I have set down my conclusions in eight Gold Mine con-cepts, each of which delivers a decisive lesson in creating and sustaining top performances. The eight concepts are:

❶ The secret is not a secret
❷ What you see is not what you get
❸ Start early or die soon
❹ We're all quitters
❺ Success is about mindset, not facilities
❻ The Godfathers

❼ Not pushing your kids is irresponsible
❽ Who wants it most

Let us return to that morning in Iten.

In no time, the Kenyans' fast pace in the thin air so high above sea level almost suffocated me, pushing my body way into the red zone. Out of politeness to the new white guy in the group they slowed their pace, but in spite of this concession, just 35 minutes after I had joined them it was all over. I stood bent double with the taste of blood in my mouth, spitting onto the verge, while the twelve Kenyans disappeared effortlessly out of sight.

I reflected on Christopher Cheboiboch's words: 'If you want to understand, you must be like a Kenyan, live like a Kenyan.' I suddenly I understood his message much more clearly.

1

The secret is not a secret

'If I had a million dollars I would close this discussion once and for all. I would lay the idea of "natural" black athletes to rest. That is not the same as saying that genes are not important, but there is no evidence that exclusive genes have been dished out to specific races.'

Dr Yannis Pitsiladis, University of Glasgow

A rotund little man stands waiting for me on the red gravel in front of St Patrick's High School. He is wearing a dark knitted jumper even though the midday sun is beating down on us and it's over 30°C. With his ruddy cheeks and a green baseball cap that barely covers the crown of his head, he looks anything but how I had imagined the world's most successful athletics coach might. Colm O'Connell has agreed to meet me here at the legendary St Patrick's High School in Iten, where everything began for him 35 years previously. In those days he was just a young Irishman whose main enjoyment in life up to that point had been 'getting pissed at Skeffington pub' while he was a student in Galway. It was certainly not on the cards that he would play a central role in the development of the planet's very best middle- and long-distance runners.

When Colm left Ireland for Kenya in February 1976 to teach at an isolated boarding school 2,800 metres up in the Rift Valley, he knew absolutely nothing about running. In fact, he had never attended an athletics meet in his life.

'I was just a geography teacher,' he says with a shrug as we sit in the St Patrick's school yard chatting in the shade.

Colm O'Connell speaking with the 1,500 metres runner
Augustine Kiprono Choge

An entirely new world welcomed Colm O'Connell when he arrived in Kenya. There was no electricity, no telephone service, no tarmac roads and, back then, no reliable running water system. A far cry from the way things had been back in Ireland. By pure chance he became involved in the school's newly initiated athletics programme as an assistant coach, although he was in no way qualified in this regard. 'I would never have been given the opportunity to become an athletics coach in England or Ireland,' he is happy to admit.

St Patrick's High School already had proud sporting traditions, especially in volleyball. The school's volleyball team did not lose a single match between 1973 and 1988. It took a few years before the school's athletics team began to perform properly but when they did, they ran fast. So fast in fact, that managed by Colm O'Connell, they won nineteen out of 21 disciplines at a national athletics meet in 1985. They did not compete in the last two disciplines.

'I learned how to coach through trial and error,' says Colm. 'Because the boys were boarders at the school I had them at my disposal 24 hours a day. This provided me with excellent conditions when it came to finding out what it took to get them to run fast.'

The entrance to St Patrick's High School in Iten

Colm's boys were superbly motivated. They had all heard of their countryman, Kipchoge Keino, the first

African athlete ever to win the Olympic 1,500 metres gold. (He did so in Mexico in 1968.) Athletics had become professionalised, and the smell of dollars had wafted its way to the Rift Valley. Over the next ten years, Colm O'Connell and St Patrick's High School would pump out one world superstar after the other.

The school yard of legends

Colm points to a tree in the school yard. On it there is a plaque embossed with the name Ibrahim Hussein.

'He was my first really good athlete,' he says.

Ibrahim Hussein was a thin lad from the Nandi tribe who came to St Patrick's at the age of fourteen. He later ended up winning the Boston Marathon three times, and was the first African ever to win the New York Marathon.

Three-times Boston Marathon champion, Ibrahim Hussein, has got his own tree at St Patrick's

The whole school yard is full of similar trees with small plaques on their trunks, each bearing the name of a great athlete who started their career at St Patrick's High School. To begin with, they planted a tree every time one of their boys won a medal at the World Championships or the Olympics. However, they soon started to run out of room, and so decided to plant just a single tree for each of the greatest winners.

A couple of metres from Ibrahim Hussein's tree stands the Birir tree. One of O'Connell's Olympic winners, Matthew Birir, brought home gold in the steeplechase at the Barcelona Olympics in 1992. As we walk through the school grounds looking at each tree in turn, I am struck by how unique the environment of St Patrick's must have been in its heyday.

'It wasn't just dominance. It was another planet,' Colm recalls, as he tells me one gripping story after another about his boys. You have to look long and hard to find a prize-winning Kenyan middle-distance runner who has not come into contact with 'Brother' O'Connell during their career. Wilson Kipketer (who, until August 2010, was 800 metres world record holder), Daniel Komen (current 3,000 metres world record holder), Asbel Kiprop, Lydia Cheromei, Susan Chepkemei, Isaac Songok, Linet Masai, Mercy Cherono, Janeth Jepkosgei, David Rudisha – you name them, Colm has trained them.

As I talk to Colm I have questions queuing up inside my head. I want to understand how it can be that this boarding school with no extraordinary facilities can achieve such staggering results. And the success of St Patrick's High School isn't where the astonishing facts end. The school is in the part of the Rift Valley that is home to the Kalenjin tribe. They make up 10 per cent of the Kenyan population. Since 1968, when Kenya began to completely dominate the Olympic steeplechase event, only a single non-Kalenjin runner has won the Olympic gold. When this sole non-Kalenjin winner, Julius Kariuki of Nyahururu, also a Kenyan, was asked about this phenomenon he said, 'It is likely that my relatives came from the Kalenjin.'

But that's not all. One of the ethnic groups under the Kalenjin tribe is the Nandi people, consisting of some 80,000 individuals. At the 2008 Olympics in Beijing, Nandi runners won the gold in both the men's and the women's 800 metres – they also won two silvers and two bronzes! What are the chances of this happening for a tribe consisting of just 80,000 people when competing against the whole of the rest of the world?

The athletic Gold Mine in the Rift Valley is one of the most sensational phenomena in the whole history of sport. We're not talking about ice hockey, rugby or baseball, all of which are regionally based sports. We are talking about a global sport, pursued professionally in almost every country in the world, and yet continually conquered by a tiny group of people all living in a 100 kilometre radius.

The running genes myth

The domination of the Kenyan runners is intimidating. In 2011 alone you find a Kenyan beside nineteen of the twenty fastest marathon times. That list includes a new world record, the winning performances from every major city marathon in 2011, and the World Championship marathon win. Not only were all the major city marathons won by Kenyans, but the course records at each were broken in the process.

More than 258 Kenyan marathon runners ran the 44.2 km race in under two hours and fifteen minutes. Britain, with a population twice the size of Kenya's, delivered only a single performance under that time. The number of top runners in Kenya seems endless, and running is not even the national sport. The runners come from a very small portion of the country where the internal competition is ruthless. This is clearly demonstrated by the case of Luke Kibet – although four months earlier he had run the eighth fastest time ever in a marathon, and was the defending world champion, he did not qualify for the Kenyan Olympic team for Beijing in 2008. (Though during the very last week before the competition he was taken on as a reserve.)

The kind of world supremacy in running that the Kenyan's enjoy strongly suggests that something more than just hard work is at play. Surely they would not be able to continually deliver the kind of performances they do without some kind of natural genetic advantage?

The same would seem to apply to Ethiopian men, who have won every single gold medal in the 10,000 metres since 1993 or, for that matter, to the West Africans sprinters responsible for 494 of the best 500 100-metre times ever run. For many years, athletes, scientists and coaches in the West have clung to the explanation that these groups of people must be equipped with special genes, perfectly designed for the specific sport in which they consistently excel.

In their attempt to explain the success of the East African medium- and long-distance runners, scientists have focused, among other things, on the Kenyans' and Ethiopians' slim calves, which they believe may be advantageous over long distances. But is this enough of an explanation? It certainly isn't as far as the Jalou people are concerned. The Jalou are a tribe in Tanzania, which borders on Kenya, and their body types and build are largely identical to their Kenyan neighbours. However, the Jalou have never produced a single top runner. This fact (along with a number of others) has raised doubts as to whether slim calves play a decisive role in the Kenyans' success at all.

Another theory is that East Africans are equipped from birth with top-of-the-line running hardware in the form of their maximum oxygen uptake, which enables them to absorb more oxygen than other people and thus work longer and harder.

But this argument also begins to waver under close inspection – Swedish physiologist Bengt Saltin has studied the physiology of East African runners and concluded that is largely identical with that of European athletes, saying, 'There is no marked disparity between the maximum oxygen uptake of an East African and a Caucasian.'

Despite these conclusions, theories about the advantages possessed by East African runners keep on popping up. Some people have tried to argue for the existence of good genes for long-distance running in the population by pointing to the absence of results in sprint events. In other words, they argue that a predisposition for long-distance running is the opposite of being predisposed to sprinting. However, when exposed to a pressure test this observation also proves untrue. As Toby Tanser writes in his book *More Fire* about Kenyan runners: 'In the fourteenth session of the men's 4×400 metre relay at the African

Championships, Kenya had five male gold medallists. In ten of the Commonwealth Games, the Kenyans have won four golds. These records remain unmatched.'

An entirely different attempt to explain the East Africans' dominance relates to the thin air 2,500 metres above sea level, the environment in which they grow up and train. Exposure to these conditions naturally increases their production of red blood corpuscles.

But if thin air is the whole explanation, why have Nepal and Mexico not produced any world-class long-distance runners?

And why is the national marathon record in Malawi more than fourteen minutes slower than the Kenyan record, when the population grows up in exactly the same type of environment as the Kalenjin people, with the Ethiopian runners training in the highlands around Addis Ababa?

A genetic explanation model of Kenyan running success has started to seem less and less plausible over time. It does not explain, for instance, why Sweden, which dominated world long-distance running in the 1940s, suddenly won the gold in the heptathlon, high jump and triple jump at the 2004 Athens Olympics. At the time not a single Swede was represented on the IAAF list of the world's 50 best long-distance runners. Are we supposed to conclude that the Swedes, in a little more than 60 years, exchanged their long-distance genes for jumping genes?

It's also not hard to see why people might get the impression that East African runners have excelled in the sport ever since it began, given their incredible performance recently. But this is simply not the case. Take, for example, the list of the top five at the marathon World Cup championships in 1999. Four of them are Europeans.

The first East African comes in ninth, even though there was no shortage of runners in Kenya and Ethiopia at the time.

Ranking	Athlete	Country	Mark
1	Antón Abel	ESP	2:13:36
2	Modica Vincenzo	ITA	2:14:03
3	Sato Nobuyuki	JPN	2:14:07
4	Novo Luis	POR	2:14:27 (SR)
5	Goffi Danilo	ITA	2:14:50

Just ten years later at the 2009 World Championships the picture is completely different. The top five has been totally taken over by Kenya and Ethiopia.

Ranking	Athlete	Country	Mark
1	Abel Kirui	KEN	2:06:54 (CR)
2	Emmanuel Kipchirchir Mutai	KEN	2:07:48
3	Tsegay Kebede	ETH	2:08:35
4	Yemane Tsegay	ETH	2:08:42
5	Robert Kipkoech Cheruiyot	KEN	

So the burning question is this: what happened during those ten years? Did the good running genes manage to emigrate from Europe, via the Mediterranean and down through the Sahara to East Africa? Unlikely. And apart from that, what has happened to the British, who used to churn out middle-distance stars such as legends David Bedford, Steve Ovett and Sebastian Coe?

These days, British men do not even manage to run into the top ten in their very own London Marathon. It was last won by a Briton in 1993 when Eamonn Martin crossed the finishing line with a time of 2:10:50. In 1985, 102 British male runners ran under the elite time of 2 hours 20 minutes for the marathon, only five managed this same feat twenty years later. British male distance running had all but disappeared. But why? Have previously efficient British genes got lost in evolution? Did British men, or other Europeans too, for that matter, suddenly start accumulating lactic acid in their muscles? Of course not. The genes of the British are as good as they ever have been.

Evidence of the fact that they can still put the Kenyans and Ethiopians in their place is to be found in Cheshire, the birthplace of Paula Radcliffe, British Queen of long-distance running and women's world Marathon record holder. If the East Africans have a perfect genetic disposition to the discipline, how can it be that a white British woman, who grew up on fish and chips, surrounded by pubs in the British lowlands, has repeatedly thrashed the Kenyans?

Yannis Pitsiladis of the University of Glasgow is one of the leading researchers in sport science. He has dedicated his career to studying the secret behind the East African long-distance runners and the West African sprinters. He is very clear indeed on his conclusions: 'There is no more evidence of a connection between specific races and specific top performance genes than there is of a connection between specific races and high intelligence. That is to say, there is no correlation whatsoever,' says Pitsiladis.

In other words: the East Africans' achievements, it transpires, are in fact much less predetermined than even the most optimistic scientists imagine.

Talent exists, but it exists everywhere

My mission here is not to close my eyes to the significance of genetics or to claim that all people on the planet have the potential to become the next Usain Bolt, Paula Radcliffe or Haile Gebrselassie. Genes are significant.

As recently as 2011, the geneticist and exercise physiologist Claude Bouchard from Laval University in Québec proved that our responsiveness to training is strongly influence by genes. Bouchard put 470 untrained volunteers through five months of training and measured their fitness levels before and after. As expected, the degree by which most people improved fell within a fairly close average range. But interestingly, in addition to these 'typical responses' Bouchard discovered considerable disparity between the level of response at the top and bottom ends. The 'low responders', the bottom 5 per cent of the sample, improved their VO$_2$max (maximal oxygen uptake) by less than 4 per cent. By contrast the high responders – the top 5 per cent – improved by 40 per cent. A difference this big is obviously crucial and it is not difficult to decide which group it would be best to recruit long-distance runners from. Some individuals simply demonstrate much greater ability to adapt to training and improve much quicker than others.

The same is true in any field. Success often lies in acknowledging that we have natural strengths and abilities that make us better equipped to excel at some things than others. Some people might be extremely extroverted and have great social skills, while others might be more introverted but have a greater potential for careful, analytical thinking. Achieving great performance is about maximising these strengths and giving people opportunities based on their natural abilities.

Back to sport. Just how crucial genetic factors are for creating world-class performers depends to a large degree on the character of the particular discipline you are looking at. Sometimes, specific genetic characteristics are particularly important. If, for instance, you are born with a lot of slow muscle fibres and very few fast ones, you will never become a world-class sprinter, no matter how hard you train. Sure, studies have shown that to a certain extent we can change slow muscle fibres to fast ones, but dramatic changes cannot be achieved. However, as long as you have a certain amount of fast muscle fibre in your basic package you still have a chance of performing competitively in this area.

The twenty-year-old French sprinter Christophe Lemaitre who, with a time of 9.92 seconds, ran his way into the exclusive club of sprinters who have done the hundred metres in under ten seconds. He ran faster than Usain Bolt did when he was twenty. Lemaitre is not a West African, but there is no doubt that his genetic profile has given him a lot of fast muscle fibres, perfectly suited to sprinting. So there are genetic profiles that match certain sports better than others, but there is no scientific evidence to suggest that there are more of the genetic profiles advantageous for sprinting among Jamaica's population of 2.8 million than anywhere else in the world.

This is precisely the conclusion that Bengt Saltin arrived at in his studies in the 1980s. When he compared some of the best Kenyan runners with some of the best Scandinavian runners, he didn't just find that the Kenyans had a smaller, lighter and slimmer leg structure. He also discovered larger amounts of haemoglobin in the blood of the Kenyans (which would enhance their endurance). The Kenyans also accumulated less lactic acid in their muscles, meaning they would succumb to fatigue more slowly. So initially, at least, one might be tempted to conclude that Kenyans as a group do have a genetic advantage in running. But that is a hasty conclusion. Although Saltin's studies confirm the hypothesis that those athletes who perform best have certain genetic advantages, this is not the same as proving that these advantages occur more frequently in Kenyans than in, for example, Swedes or Britons.

As Saltin puts it, 'We have no idea whether a specific "running gene" exists, but what we do know is that the athletes who perform the best have a genetic advantage and that training of the body is a key factor. What is crucial is the activation of these genes. However, we also know that genetic advantages cannot be traced to specific ethnic groups.'

In other words, if we randomly selected 100 people on the street in Kingston, Jamaica, and took them to a laboratory to examine their muscle fibre type and genetic profile, we would not find more people with the potential to become super-sprinters then we would if we gathered 100 people off the street in Birmingham in England which has about the same population as Kingston. To put it another way, although innate talent exists, it does so everywhere.

The concept of 'good enough'

Unfortunately, the debate about innate talent and the significance of genetics in top performance is often highly theoretical and difficult to get to grips with. The real question therefore is this: how can we use the insight that innate talent exists, but that it exists everywhere, in a hands-on, practical way?

As far as I can see there is one crucial lesson to be learnt for all managers, coaches and teachers who try to identify and release talent: genetics cannot predict who will become an Olympic medallist. All it can do is predict who is certain to *never* win a medal.

Usain Bolt was born with enough fast muscle fibres to become a world-class sprinter. Haile Gebrselassie was certainly a 'high responder' to training. Both men have genetic profiles that have allowed them to achieve high levels of performance. The raw material was there – they were 'good enough'. There are bound to have been an awful lot of other people who could have emulated their achievements; the reason these unknown others never became as good as Usain and Haile does not have anything to do with their genes, but with a whole series of other factors such as motivation, their coaches and the quality of their training.

Eddie Coyle, director of the Human Performance Laboratory at the University of Texas, Austin, has thoroughly tested the seven-times Tour de France winner Lance Armstrong since he was twenty years old, both physiologically and biologically. He draws the same conclusions: 'To be the best cyclist on the planet, you don't have to be superhuman in any of the necessary genetic components, but you can't be weak in any of them.'

In this way, innate talent becomes a sort of primary sorting mechanism. Or, to put it another way, being 2.10 metres tall doesn't necessarily mean you can become an NBA player, but it is helpful. If, on the other hand, you're 1.75 metres tall your chances are dramatically decreased. However, the shortest man to ever play in the NBA is Tyrone Bogues, at only 1.60 metres tall. He used his height to his advantage, gaining a reputation as a great passer, ball-stealer and one of the fastest players on the court. So Bogues demonstrates that being 'good enough' to play in the NBA is probably not as closely related to height as we might assume. At the same time we have to admit that in many respects, he is exceptional.

What being 'good enough' means depends on the nature and the demands of the discipline in question. Take a business leader, for example. You'll have a hard time becoming a great leader without a strong sense of empathy and the ability to deal with other people psychologically. Without those skills you might become a good administrator, but you'll never excel as a leader. In any discipline there is a minimum of natural skill you must have in order to be able to become really, really good. Talent is the access ticket to the game, though it's not the decisive factor.

As a general rule of thumb, in the world of sport we can conclude that the simpler the sport, the greater the role played by genes. Sprinting, which is a relatively simple discipline, has only limited genetic requirements (you have to have a lot of fast muscle fibres), while football, a relatively complex discipline, opens the way for many more genetic variations (you can, for instance, have a lot of slow muscle fibres but still reach the top because you think quickly or have good technique: you can compensate).

Reaching the minimum requirements to excel is considerably more difficult in sprinting than in football because it's harder to compensate for not having a critical mass of fast twitch muscle fibres. This is not the same as saying that

you can't improve if you don't meet the minimum requirements. You can. But you will never be world class without
meeting them.

If you don't have enough stretch in your foot joints and
rotation in your hips at age seven you will never become a
talented ballet dancer. You will never become a competent
counsellor if you do not possess a certain amount of emotional intelligence. If you score less than 100 in an IQ test
it is highly unlikely you will ever be admitted to Harvard.
That is not to say that you cannot become a better dancer,
more empathetic or a more rigourous thinker, but you will
never be among the very best at what you do. Innate talent
is not the decisive factor, but it is the entry ticket to the
game.

As Dennis Johnson, the former 100 metre world record
holder and Jamaican sprint coach, told me one night at a
hotel in Kingston: 'To be a good sprinter you have got to
have been born with a certain amount of fast muscle fibres.
In that sense great sprinters are born. But a lot of people
meet these minimum requirements. If you selected a group
of sixteen-year-old British boys with enough fast muscle
fibres, I could get them to run the hundred metres in ten
seconds flat within four years. It's very simple. Even if you
don't have the necessary fast muscle fibres you can improve
enormously. You won't become world class, but you'll be
good.'

The concept of capitalisation

It is here that the brilliant American scientist James Flynn
comes into the picture. Flynn has developed the concept of 'capitalisation', which describes the percentage of

human potential in a given community that is successfully unlocked. In other words, the percentage of people capable of achieving something who actually end up achieving it. One can call it a kind of TQ (talent quotient). Any society, organisation or individual has a TQ, which is an expression of the ability to realise existing potential. Unlike IQ, which is a static intelligence, TQ is a dynamic – it does not concern itself with whether or not talent exists. It does, and is found everywhere. Instead, TQ measures the ability to bring it into play, to capitalise on it and to convert it into actual results.

James Flynn has looked at the capitalisation rates of various occupations in the US. He has assessed, for example, what percentage of American men intellectually capable of holding top-tier managerial jobs actually end up getting those kinds of jobs. The number is surprisingly low, around 60 per cent. This is an expression of quite a low TQ, indicating a lot of room for improvement.

TQ is what company executives, teachers and sports coaches who want to develop top performance should measure themselves by. It is not a question of whether talent exists or not. There is a lot of talent out there, and it is frequently standing in front of your very eyes. The question is how good we are at capitalising on that potential. How many people who can be really good at what they do actually get that good?

We have seen that Jamaica, for example, is obviously outstanding in capitalising on people's potential for sprinting. Again, it's not that you will find more people in Kingston per 100 inhabitants with the potential to become world-class sprinters than you will find per 100 people anywhere else. It's just that the percentage of those people who actually end up as sprinters is much higher in Jamaica because they have a system that identifies potential and grows it.

There are formal elements to this system – Jamaican children start competing in athletics at the age of two or three. Several kindergartens even have an athletics coach and from the age of six. The kids have the opportunity to run at the National Stadium in Kingston in front of a large crowd. Sprinting is on the school curriculum. Everybody runs for their school, and this means that every Jamaican boy and girl is tested for their potential as a sprinter.

I met the sprint coach Glen Mills – known as the architect of Usain Bolt's success – after a training session at the University of West India. He explained: 'People tend to underrate the fact that those who have the potential to become a good sprinter end up actually being good sprinters in Jamaica. In other countries they might study technology or play another sport. If Usain Bolt had grown up in the United States he would probably not have become a sprinter, but a basketball player or perhaps even a wide receiver in American football. He would have gone in an entirely different direction.'

Exactly the same applies to the runners in Kenya. Iten in Kenya has an extremely low TQ when it comes to developing software engineers, but an enormously high TQ as far as the development of long-distance runners is concerned. This is not because there is more innate running talent there than in any other country, but because the system there rounds up all the potential world stars and gives them a unique training environment in which to flourish. Think about it: here we have 1,000 athletes, all of whom grew up at least 2,500 metres above sea level. They push each other every day to the extreme and are ultra-motivated by the desire to create a better life for themselves and their families. They have all run ever since they were small, and are able to train side-by-side with the very best runners in the world, surrounded by running culture and running legends. They basically do nothing but run, eat and sleep. Where else in the world could you find those conditions?

Gold Mines must be created, not discovered

The deeper I reached into the six Gold Mines, the more it became clear to me that success cannot be traced back to an exclusive genetic design. As Dennis Johnson expressed it: 'I would like to tell the whole world that there is no magic. No special nose or long ears, it's just normal people that run fast.'

The evidence that invalidates the exclusive gene theory is convincing in practical as well as scientific terms. It sends a crystal clear, motivating message to anyone who wants to create a Gold Mine of high performance: this is achievable. It has more to do with your ability to capitalise on the talent that indisputably exists than anything else. To put it another way, Gold Mines are not going to be discovered. They are going to be uncovered. Ninety-nine per cent of the resources you need to succeed are already in your building.

This is the same message that the Godfather of Kenyan running, Colm O'Connell, serves up in his own peculiar way at Iten's only cafe, the Keryo View, where we had agreed to meet a couple of hours before I boarded the plane to head home to Europe.

'So, have you discovered what the secret is?' asks Colm, taking a sip of his coffee.

'The question is whether there is a secret at all,' I respond. Colm O'Connell sits there silently for a few seconds, looking out over the rolling green landscape of the Rift Valley.

'The secret is that there is no secret. And we won't tell you what it is because there is none. But we'll keep pushing you to make you think there is,' he says. Then he laughs out loud, before concluding: 'People make a big mistake when they believe that the discussion is about good and bad genes. In reality it's all about belief. What do you think is possible? There is no more running talent in Kenya than in Britain, but the British believe there is. And if you believe you are limited by your genes you will probably never invest what it takes to become good. You've excluded yourself. Here in Iten nobody is in doubt, because if you don't believe in yourself in Kenya, nobody else will, and belief doesn't cost you anything. Everybody can afford it.'

What your should never forget about TALENT

1. Talent is not race-linked. It is everywhere. And I really mean **everywhere**!

2. Genetics can't tell us who will be a star performer. At best it can tell us who will certainly never be. Good genes might be the entry ticket to the game of world-class performance, but they not the decisive factor for who will win. Don't overrate the importance of in-born talent.

3. Talent is not something static; it's not something that you either have or you don't, and if you don't you're out of the game. It must be understood dynamically. For example, many women in the world sing better than Madonna. Plenty of women are better looking as well. But Madonna has managed to administer what she has at her disposal and to put it into action. This is what constitutes true talent.

4. Leave it to the scientists to discuss what percentage of world-class performance is dependent on genetics. Your job is to believe that nothing is impossible and to act as if inborn talent doesn't play a role at all. In other words: stop crying and wishing for better genes. Start dealing with what you've got!

What you see is not what you get

'It isn't difficult to identify talent like Usain Bolt. Anybody could see that he had huge potential when he was sixteen. The real challenge is to identify the potential in something currently ordinary that hasn't flourished yet.'

Stephen Francis, head coach of
the MVP Track and Field Club

Many people were amazed when, on a June day in 2005, at the Athens Olympic Stadium, the 22-year-old Jamaican Asafa Powell sprinted his way into the history books, setting a new world record in the 100 metres. The surprise was not so much that Tim Montgomery's world record of 9.78 seconds had finally fallen, but that it was a virtual unknown who toppled it. Unlike his countryman, Usain Bolt – who already as a thirteen year old was predicted to set new standards in the sprint distances – nobody expected very much at all of Asafa Powell.

Only three years earlier, Asafa was just another Jamaican teenager wandering about Kingston trying to find a place to train. His best time for the hundred metres was

10.8 seconds, which he ran in a semi-final during his high school's championships. This was not nearly fast enough for somebody to want to invest in his future. So how could an unknown Jamaican develop in just a few years from a mediocre sprinter to the fastest man on the planet?

It would soon transpire that Asafa Powell's world record was the first symptom of the sprint revolution that was seething just below the surface of global athletics. It broke out in full three years later at the 2008 Beijing Olympics. Here, the Jamaican sprinters annihilated the competition, winning an unheard of eleven medals (six gold, three silver and two bronze). They set three world records and four Olympic records. When Shelly-Ann Fraser, Veronica Campbell-Brown and Sherone Simpson took the gold, silver and bronze in the women's 100 metres, the demonstration of power was complete. The world was incredulous and its gaze was fixed firmly on one tiny island in the Atlantic.

Unknown world stars

It is old news that the Jamaicans regularly show up among the world's fastest sprinters. Over the last 50 years, they have regularly received medals in the sprint distances at major championships. And at the fifteen Olympic games held during the period 1948–2004, Jamaica won an average of a little under three medals per games, which is not bad at all for a nation of only 2.4 million people. In this light, the medals in Beijing shine even brighter. They show an almost 400 per cent improvement in performance over four years. But was this just a one-hit wonder?

Twelve months later, at the 2009 World Championships in Berlin, Jamaica proved beyond doubt that it was not.

Again, the Jamaicans outperformed the rest of the world's athletes, and with even greater superiority than in Beijing the previous year. A total of thirteen medals (seven gold, four silver and two bronze) crowned the Jamaicans the undisputed kings (and queens) of sprint. If the world was incredulous after the Beijing Olympics, now they were completely stupified. Even the United States, traditionally the major sprinting nation, was left in the dust by this display of Jamaican reggae power. The sprint revolution was now a reality and if there was one question the championships in Berlin begged, it was this: how had Jamaica developed in just a few years from being merely a decent sprinting nation to the world's undisputed ruler?

The yam effect

No end of people have tried to explain Jamaica's turbo-charged magic. One of the more entertaining explanations is referred to as the 'the yam effect'. After Usain Bolt's win in the 100 metres at the Beijing Olympics, his father, Wellesley, told reporters that the secret to his son's success was the potato-like vegetable, the yam. More specifically, the yellow yam, which is said to be the favourite yam in Jamaica and which is apparently Bolt junior's favourite food.

Others have attempted to attribute the Jamaican's success to their shared history as slaves more than 175 years ago. This, the theory goes, gave them the aggressiveness, ferocity and strength it takes to run like human cheetahs.

A third explanation, as naive as the yam-effect, is that the Jamaicans have long ring fingers – this, in some way or other, is supposed to help them to run faster.

These increasingly implausible theories simply reflect the world's astonishment at the seemingly equally implausible results Jamaica's sprinters have delivered. But it does not end there. Their achievements become even more impressive when one realises that the stories of many Jamaican athletes are similar to that of Asafa Powell.

Take the world champion and Olympic champion in the 100 metres for women, Shelly-Ann Fraser; or the Olympic silver medallist in the 100 metres, Sherone Simpson; or the world champion in the 110 metres hurdles, Brigitte Foster-Hylton. Until a few years ago, they were all athletes who had been written off because they had not made the grade.

Jamaica's demonstration of power is not about a long string of superb talents finally showing their worth. It is about unknown sprinters suddenly breaking out as world stars. And so I set off to explore the enclaves of Jamaican sprinting. My purpose was to solve the mystery of this tiny nation turning completely overlooked sprinters – considered to be grade C or D at best – into Olympic winners and world champions in just a few years.

We are going to beat the American high school coaches

One September day in 1999, nearly ten years before the Jamaican blitzkrieg in Beijing, two men, Bruce James and Stephen Francis, were sitting in a flat in Kingston reaching a decision that would come to shake the entire athletics world. The two went way back – as a high school athlete, James had been coached at Wolmer's Boys' School by Francis, who was only four years his senior. Together they improved James's time in the 400 metres enough for him to win a track scholarship to Florida State University in the United States. Francis also went to the US, where he took an MBA in finance at the University of Michigan. He planned to use it as a springboard into the corporate world, and when he came back to Jamaica he joined the international firm KPMG. But he missed athletics. His great passion for coaching was tugging at him. He began to think about returning to the world of athletics, and to speculate about the possibility of doing something very special there.

Strange as it may seem, Francis was never an athlete himself – he arrived at his expertise through reading. To begin with he spend a lot of time at the library in Kingston and then, as he began to earn more money, he started buying and importing books on the subject of coaching and improving athletic performance.

After a few months of consideration, Stephen Francis decided to resign from his job in order to coach full time. That is how he came to be sitting there with his old friend Bruce James, planning what we know today as the biggest sprint revolution of the last 50 years. The basis of this revolution was simple – Francis and James wondered why Jamaican athletes always had to go to the United States in order to succeed. Why not train them at home in Jamaica?

The general conviction was that Jamaican high school coaches were nowhere near as good as American coaches. When it came to athletics, the Jamaicans were simply babysitters for the Americans – when the best Jamaican athletes left high school, these sublime American coaches would take over and transform them from merely good athletes into extraordinary athletes. There was plenty of evidence that this model worked. As far as everyone was concerned, the way forward was via the US. This had been the case for Olympic medallists like Grace Jackson, Merlene Ottey, Don Quarrie and many others. All had been given a scholarship to an American university and subsequently won medals at the World Championships and the Olympics. These examples seemed to emphasise that the system worked – and if the system isn't broken, then why fix it?

But Bruce James and Stephen Francis were convinced that there was a better way. Francis had a tremendous record of training young Jamaican athletes to the standard required to get a scholarship to the US, but he felt as though they never really realised their full potential once they got there. He expected to see them at the World Championships and the Olympics, but it never happened. In fact, he had never been particularly impressed by what the American coaches achieved with Jamaican athletes. Given this he began to consider the possibility of creating a new training environment on Jamaica – one that would pump out superstars.

So on that September day in 1999 James and Francis decided to found the MVP (Maximising Velocity and Power) Track and Field Club. James became president and Francis head coach. Together they launched the project with the words: 'Gentlemen, we shall show the American college coaches that we can do the job ourselves here in Jamaica.'

Barefoot sprinters

The MVP Track and Field Club was a project founded against all odds. People in Jamaica shook their heads at the level of its ambition. Francis and James were called unrealistic dreamers. It was also almost impossible for them to attract the best, most talented sprinters. Not only did training take place on a diesel-scorched grass field; they couldn't even afford to buy running shoes for their athletes. As a result, many of them trained in bare feet. Added to this was the fact that Francis, the head coach, had never been an elite sprinter himself and had only coached youth athletes. They quite simply had no results to show.

So rather than working with the top athletes in Jamaica, they had to make do with those who were willing to train with them, and the only people willing to stay in Jamaica to train were those who the Americans had turned away. Francis began to look for young sprinters who were good enough in his eyes but who had not been deemed good enough for a scholarship to the United States.

The first athlete at the MVP Track and Field Club was a 25-year-old Jamaican woman. Although she had been to university in the United States, she had never quite had a breakthrough and had now returned home. She was the perfect candidate. Her name was Brigitte Foster-Hylton.

Brigitte Foster-Hylton training on the grass tracks at the MVP Track and Field Club in Kingston

Just a year later, under the guidance of Stephen Francis, her performance had improved so much that she managed to qualify for the 100 metres hurdles at the Sydney Olympics, where she crossed the line in eighth place.

James and Francis were ecstatic. They had taken an athlete who had been written off and trained her to become one of the best in the world. They felt they had made their decisive breakthrough. In actual fact, nobody seemed to take much notice of the story of Brigitte Foster-Hylton. At the same time, the MVP Track and Field Club was seriously low on funds. Francis was forced to sell his car and was in such a poor financial state that he was unable to get a credit card. He couldn't afford even electricity because he needed all his spare money to make sure that his athletes didn't starve; many of them couldn't afford to buy their own food. Despite the inspirational story of Brigitte Foster-Hylton, the MVP was on the verge of collapse.

In late 2000 Stephen Francis heard about the 19-year-old Asafa Powell through a friend. As we saw earlier in the chapter, Powell's results were far from impressive – his best was 10.8 seconds in the semi-final of the High School Championships. Moreover, he came from a school that nobody in Jamaica knew, and which did not have a well-developed athletics programme. But Stephen Francis recognised his potential. He thought if he could get the lad to train in a structured manner, he could probably get him to go a long way. Within a week of Stephen Francis seeing him run, Asafa Powell was standing on the MVP training track.

Somehow, the MVP Track and Field Club scraped along until 14 June 2005. It was then that the breakthrough came. At the Olympic stadium in Athens, Asafa Powell crossed the line in 9.77 seconds (a new world record), and so became the fastest man on earth. How could almost everyone, the Americans included, have overlooked Powell's potential? How come only Stephen Francis could see it?

The MVP effect

Asafa's world record was precisely what the MVP Track and Field Club needed and since that day they have never looked back. At the Beijing Olympics, MVP's eight athletes brought home nine medals, five of them gold, setting one world record and one Olympic record along the way. They repeated the trick at the World Championships in Berlin – Francis's eight sprinters, in an out-of-this-world demonstration of power, won eleven medals, six of them gold. One of those gold winners was the MVP's first athlete, Brigitte Foster-Hylton. This total domination has since become known as the MVP Effect.

Today, the MVP Track and Field Club is the indisputably the world's most successful athletics club, and is the reason that Jamaica leads the world in the sprint distances. Stephen Francis and Bruce James are the architects of this sprint revolution. Remove the MVP athletes' performances from the equation and Jamaica performs precisely as it always has done. Only two of the eleven medals the country won at the Beijing Olympics were won by non-MVP runners.

In other words, to understand the secret behind the Jamaican super-sprinters you have to understand how Stephen Francis thinks. The success of the MVP athletes has nothing to do with genes, yams or traits arising from suffering the atrocities of slavery. We must realise that first and foremost it can be traced back to Francis's ability to spot

Asafa Powell at the MVP Track and Field Club's training ground

potential in a sprinter that everyone else overlooks. When it comes to spotting talent, he has totally changed the game, rethinking all the traditional methods and assumptions.

Stay clear of 'can't miss' athletes

It is 5.30 in the morning and I am standing in front of the MVP Track and Field's training ground in Kingston. The smooth contours of some runners moving silently through the dark are just visible behind the fence. I can see about 40 athletes on the grass, once my eyes have accustomed themselves to the dark.

The silence is suddenly broken by a big black BMW which drives at speed towards the fence and stops just behind me. A large, round man dressed in a loose T-shirt gets out. With slow, short steps he moves his wide body towards the hole in the fence that is the official entrance to the training ground. This is Stephen Francis. 'Welcome to MVP,' he says, offering his large hand.

Like everything else on the training ground, Stephen Francis does not resemble what he actually is; his BMW is the only obvious sign of his success. He simply arrives here every morning at 5.30, sets up his folding chair on the grass and proceeds to oversee the training of the world's best sprinters in his deep, booming voice.

Stephen Francis is a man of few, though meaningful, words. He answers when you ask a question, otherwise he says nothing. At home in Jamaica he divides opinion. Some call him a genius; others call him greedy and arrogant. But nobody can deny the list of super-athletes he has created, which makes him the world's most successful sprint coach. And one of the most thought-provoking things about

Stephen Francis, head coach of the MVP Track and Field Club

Francis is the fact that he has never sprinted himself, but trained as a statistician. He sees this as an advantage. In his words: 'I think that I have an extra perspective as a coach because I have not been active myself. Many athletics coaches are themselves former athletes. I have taken the steps to understand what they know, but I don't believe that they have taken the steps to understand what I know.'

And we should keep in mind not only the incredible results of the MVP Track and Field Club but also the story of previous mediocrity which so many of its athletes share. Nobody was a star before they came here. Many of them had not even won a medal in the Jamaican High School Championships. Olympic medallists like Shelly-Ann Fraser, Sherone Simpson, Shericka Williams and, by no means least, the former world record holder in the 100 metres,

Sherone Simpson and Shelly-Ann Fraser after training at MVP

Asafa Powell. All of them were unknown athletes with no real hope of a successful career, until they came under Stephen Francis's wing.

'I love to work with people who are hungry for a second chance. I love to prove that people made a mistake. That other stuff bores me,' he tells me, before blowing loudly on his whistle, at which his athletes jog in small groups towards where he sits planted on his folding chair. The sun has just come out and Francis has donned his sunglasses. Moments later the athletes are crowding around him. I quickly spot three Olympic gold winners amid the throng.

'I stay clear of those I call "can't miss" athletes as a matter of principle. Instead I look for those with the greatest development potential,' Francis finishes.

Talent that whispers

In his excellent book *The Rare Find*, the business journalist George Anders distinguishes between two types of talent: that which shouts and that which whispers. Usain Bolt is a perfect example of talent that shouts – what Stephen Francis calls a 'can't miss' athlete.

At the age of fifteen Bolt was the youngest junior champion ever. He performed outstandingly, and obviously possessed tremendous potential.

'Athletes like Usain Bolt [100m and 200m World Record Holder] and Veronica Campbell-Brown [Olympic 200 metres champion] were also the very best when they were juniors. The fact that they run very fast isn't news. You would have to be half blind not to recognise their class,' Francis explains to me.

Asafa Powell, on the other hand, is a perfect example

of talent that whispers, and the same applies to Shelly-Ann Fraser, Brigitte Foster-Hylton, Sherone Simpson and Shericka Williams. All of them possessed tremendous potential but went unnoticed because this was not obviously apparent in their performance at the time.

Talent that whispers is found in all walks of life, and is far more common than we might believe. Take, for example, the two FC Barcelona star players, Andres Iniesta and Xavi, who helped win the World Cup for Spain and brought the Champions League Trophy and the Spanish championships home to Barcelona. When they were on the youth team aged twelve and fourteen they won nothing, and as eighteen and nineteen year olds they had lost more matches than they had won.

And the best basketball player of all time, Michael Jordan, was not deemed good enough to play on his high school team at the age of sixteen.

The former world 800 metres champion and world record holder Wilson Kipketer was nowhere near the best athlete at the boarding school he attended in Kenya.

And perhaps the best example of all is the Brazilian football legend Ronaldo Luíz Nazario de Lima. In 1996 he walked onto the stage to receive his FIFA World Player of the Year award at the a gala dinner in Zürich. Bathed in the flashlights of the world media, the nineteen-year-old Brazilian received the Golden Ball as the youngest player ever to do so, following an outstanding season at FC Barcelona. His performance led football experts to compare him with legends like Diego Maradona and his fellow Brazilian Pelé.

However, nobody could have imagined Ronaldo's success in their wildest dreams if they had seen his circumstances just four years earlier. He had been drifting clubless around Brazil looking for a contract. Flamengo turned the fifteen-year-old Ronaldo away at the door because they were not sufficiently interested to be willing to pay for his bus fare to and from training (about a dollar for a return ticket). The reason they gave was that he was too small and slight. He was subsequently rejected by several other Brazilian clubs for the same reason, until he was finally accepted at Cruzeiro in the city of Belo Horizonte, some 500 km from Rio de Janeiro.

In fact, more or less the same script seems to have been played out in the lives of some of the most successful individuals, and not just in sport but in areas ranging from investing and politics to publishing, music and advertising. Many of today's biggest stars in those fields were hardly noticed at first. One of the most outstanding examples is J.K. Rowling, author of the Harry Potter series, which has sold more than 450 million copies worldwide. She was rejected time after time by publishers until Bloomsbury eventually took a chance on her – and you can bet they're glad that they did! Paul Cézanne, Elvis Presley, Michael Jordan, Ray Charles and Charles Darwin were all thought to have little potential in their chosen fields. In other words: the world has many 'Asafa Powells' in it.

How to spot a superstar

In retrospect we laugh at the football coaches who refused to pay Ronaldo's bus ticket and the college coaches who repeatedly rejected Asafa Powell. How could anyone reject point-blank a player who four years later would be voted the world's best? How can you overlook the potential of one of the fastest people on earth? What a blooper. But were they foolish or incompetent, or is trying to predict future accomplishments just mission impossible?

Probably the coaches were right about Ronaldo and Asafa – in terms of their skills at the time. They were not yet performing at even close to the level which would one day make them famous. After all, there was a time when Asafa Powell was just an ordinary guy.

And that's just the point: how do you spot the potential in something that looks ordinary? Fundamentally, it is a prediction problem. What does potential which has not yet found expression look like? And what do we look for when potential does not manifest itself in current top performance?

Figuring out how to catch those early stirrings of promise is quite rightly an obsession for any ambitious organisation, whether it's an advertising agency, a baseball team or a music academy. They all want to win the war for talent, and nobody wants to walk past the next superstar. But how do you spot a superstar who is not yet a superstar? What does talent that whispers look like?

What you see is not always what you get

The answer to those questions is worth a lot of money. All over the world, in every field from academia to music, millions of dollars and thousands of hours are being spent on identifying high-potential performers early on. The harsh truth, however, is that the vast majority of these talent-ID programmes use ineffective methods. In many cases they are no better than drawing lots. As Capital One's CEO, Richard Fairbank, put it several years ago, 'At most companies, people spend 2 per cent of their time recruiting and 75 per cent managing their recruiting mistakes.'

Take the NFL (the National Football League in America), for example, the crème de la crème of talent identification science.

The NFL Scouting Combine is held in April every year. It is a sort of mini-camp where NFL coaches and managers meet to assess the nation's greatest talent. In simple terms, the idea is to invite North America's 300 best college players to Indianapolis where they are then tested in every aspect of the game – how high they can jump, how much weight they can lift, how fast they can run and so on. All these tests are designed to produce an accurate picture of the players' true potential, and every bit of available data is analysed. The whole thing is transmitted live on American TV. Millions of dollars are at stake, meaning that managers and coaches demand extremely reliable information – they need it in order to have the best chance of correctly predicting the stars of the future. This is what the NFL Scouting Combine is all about.

But there's a problem: every year, the NFL coaches and scouts manage to get it absolutely wrong. In fact, out of the 40 top-rated combine performers over the past four years, only half are still *in the league.*

A good example of how ineffective the techniques used by the NFL can be is the famous Wonderlic Cognitive Ability Test, which is used by the NFL Scouting Combine to test potential quarterbacks. To be a quarterback in the NFL you have two possess well-developed cognitive skills and be a quick, confident decision-maker. You have to be able to remember thousands of game situations, and you have to spend hundreds of hours studying attack openings and strategies. It seems to make good sense to apply an intelligence test to candidates, but it turns out that among the seven players noted for the worst performances in the Wonderlic test in the history of the NFL Scouting Combine, we find two of the best quarterbacks ever – Terry Bradshaw and Dan Marino. In other words, the test appears to be useless as an indicator of potential as a quarterback, to put it mildly.

So it seems to be exceptionally difficult to spot super-stars, and we can find frustrated talent assessors in practically any field. It is not just in the sporting world that money is routinely wagered on draft picks that end up being hugely disappointing. Many corporations spend millions attracting new hotshot executives, only to end up writing even larger severance cheques a few years later in order to get rid of their failures. And think about the entertainment industry – sales bins are bursting with merchandise, CDs and movies which were supposed to have attracted millions of fans but which never made their mark.

The art of identifying the extraordinary – talent that will consistently drive exceptional productivity and give lasting results – is an extremely tough discipline. In desper-ation at the many poor guesses made during the last dec-ade, we have made talent identification more sophisticated and complex than ever before. We have huge job databases at our disposal. Specialist software allows us to sort and prioritise skills in an instant, and as if that were not enough, we can also choose between numerous psychological tests which are supposed to tell us about candidates' reaction patterns, personalities and chances of success. But despite the availability of all these technical aids, there is little indi-cation that we have improved in any way when it comes to identifying potential. It seems to remain an unsolvable mystery.

Back in Kingston, Jamaica, Stephen Francis is laughing into his beard. His track record bears witness to an uncanny skill to see potential that nobody else can. It is interesting to consider whether Stephen Francis would be better at spotting a software engineer than many software companies. Whether he would be better at spotting the potential of teachers than most schools. Whatever the field, everyone basically wants to achieve the same thing: to find the superstars before anybody else does.

Step back from the details of Stephen Francis' methods, and it's possible to discern a few big ideas that can apply almost anywhere. Here are the four principles to spot talent that whispers.

1. It's not about the performance – it's about the story behind the performance

When we try to spot up-and-coming superstars, it is not that the methods we typically use are poor at assessing the things they are meant to assess. The problem is that measuring people's performance is the wrong way to approach the task, and it's especially likely to overlook talent that whispers. If you want to assess whether a person has what it takes to be among the world's elite in their field, it is no good looking at what we can see here and now: current performance. To spot real potential you must be able to look beyond that and identify the complex, multi-faceted qualities that help someone learn and keep on learning, to break barriers and to work beyond inevitable plateaus.

Imagine an iceberg.

Icebergs float on the ocean with only about 10 per cent of their mass visible above the surface; the remaining 90 per cent is concealed beneath the waves. Think of the upper 10 per cent of the iceberg as current performance. The 90 per cent beneath the water is the currently unseen potential. It is there that the answers lie – in the mindset, the motivations and the values that form the basis of the current performance you are witnessing. That means that you will also find the seeds of development potential there. None of this can be measured with a stopwatch or a tape measure. It's far more subtle and complex, and requires that you do not allow yourself to be distracted by current performance. It is precisely this skill which Stephen Francis possesses in such abundance, and which has been the basis of the sprint revolution at the MVP Track and Field Club.

According to Stephen Francis, one of the great misconceptions about talent identification arises from our conviction that current high performance automatically equals a great potential and that current average performance equals low potential. Current performance *can* certainly be a good indicator of potential but this is not always the case.

One way to understand the difference between performance and potential is to look at them in isolation, using a classic nine-box matrix like the one below. The X (horizontal) axis assesses current performance – the results the person delivers here and now – and the Y (vertical) axis assesses potential – a prediction of future talent, possible achievements and capabilities. By combining their places on the X and Y axes we can locate an individual in a particular box on the grid.

Performance			
High performance Low potential	High performance Average potential	High performance High potential
Average performance Low potential	Average performance Average potential	Average performance High potential
Low performance Low potential	Low performance Average potential	Low performance High potential

Potential

Let us return for a moment to the phenomenal Usain Bolt, who is one of those athletes who was spectacular even in childhood. He's been winning competitions his entire live, and still does. In our matrix, athletes like him are characterised as high performance/high potential. Asafa Powell, on the other hand, demonstrated nothing extraordinary in his early performances, even when he first started training at MVP. He would be placed in the average performance/ high potential box. Spotting the potential of someone like Asafa is much more difficult – you have to look beyond your initial snap judgement of the person.

This is precisely why Stephen Francis's methods concentrate on people's potential to rise beyond what they have done to date and not only on their current performance. What is important to him is not performance in itself, but what caused it and the story that lies behind it. Because of this, one of the key areas Francis looks at when trying to assess talent is training history. This is based on the idea that if you know an athlete's past, you'll have a greater chance of evaluating the possibilities for future. As Francis explains: 'Imagine that you see a guy running the hundred metres in 10.2 seconds as a nineteen year old. Then you see another nineteen year old running the distance in 10.6. Everything seems to be screaming at you that you should choose the one who runs 10.2. But if you're good, you will know that the guy who ran the distance in 10.6 may have even greater potential. Imagine, for instance, that the 10.2 guy is came from a very professional and qualified training environment, while the 10.6 guy basically trained on his own. I look very closely at athletes' training histories. The better an athlete is without having a good training history, the greater the potential that exists.'

The exact same principle applies in fields other than sport. Lots of factors can influence the performance level of a business team as well as for an individual. Luck is one of them. Although sustained high performance may arise from skilful management or other valuable, rare and intimitable qualities, it can also be product of luck. Among other factors affecting results are unique circumstances, conjunctures, available resources and so on. If you deeply understand what role these factors have played in achieving a given result, you'll have a much more solid knowledge on which to base your judgements about the real potential of a team or individual. If you really take the time to understand the story driving the numbers in front of you, you'll suddenly start seeing the patterns that will allow you to find undervalued talent both inside and outside an organisation. This is what characterises every outstanding leader, whether they are a coach, entrepreneur or teacher.

This approach is how Stephen Francis found Asafa Powell, who at the age of seventeen ran the 100m in 10.8 seconds. He'd been to a poor high school with a bad coach and hadn't trained much at all. The training he had done consisted of him going over to G.C. Foster College in Kingston, looking at the way they trained, then going home and doing the same thing.

'This told me that Asafa probably had considerable underexploited potential,' Francis explains.

Talent apartheid

We can find one of the worst examples of staring blindly at performance and overlooking the story behind in football. An interesting pattern will appear before your eyes if you spend an evening studying the 300 players who were selected for the 2010 FIFA World Cup. 32.4 per cent of the players were born in January, February or March. 25.2 per cent of the players were born in April, May or June. Only 21.5 per cent were born in July, August or September and

21 per cent in October, November or December. In other words, the World Cup is a big party for boys born early in the year. In disciplines like ice hockey and tennis, this pattern also flourishes. The figures speak for themselves, but what lies at the roots of this strange trend?

The explanation is simple. To understand the reasons for the pattern we have to go back in time to the point where these players were identified as talented, to the moment the coach said: 'I believe in you. You have talent, and for that reason you will have a special chance to realise it.'

This moment usually occurs for young footballers between the ages of eleven and fifteen. By this point they have been divided into year groups; they play together with children who were born in the same year. Now, try for a moment to think back to the class you were in at school when you were fourteen years old, or perhaps a sports team you played on. What were you like? Were you big and strong, or were you small and slight? Were you an early or late developer compared to others the same age?

My guess is that in retrospect you will remember prominent cognitive, physical and emotional differences between the oldest and the youngest fourteen year old. A rule of thumb is that there can be as much as three years' developmental difference between children born in the space of one year, if you look at them during adolescence. In other words, an early-developing eleven year old might be at the same level of physical maturity as an average fourteen year old, but so might a late-developing seventeen year old.

Imagine what this difference means to current performance in a physical sport like football. Who do you think will be most dominant on the pitch? And who do you think most coaches will notice? The answer is obvious. The phenomenon has been dubbed 'relative age' and is the reason that players born in January, February and March are consistently over-represented in the world's football teams. People assume they are spotting talent, while in actual fact what they spot is physical superiority due to early development. In other words: *what you see is not always what you get*. Any parent, coach or teacher should be aware that just one single judgement that focuses solely on current performance without an understanding of the underlying reasons for that performance can have dramatic consequences for someone's future path and potential.

High performance Low potential	High performance Average potential	High performance High potential
Average performance Low potential	Average performance Average potential	Average performance High potential
Low performance Low potential	Low performance Average potential	Low performance High potential

Performance (vertical axis) — *Potential* (horizontal axis)

Let us return for a moment to the nine-box matrix. Many footballers born early in the year, who as a result are more likely to develop early, can be categorised in the top left-hand corner: high performance/low potential. They are good right now, but this often doesn't indicate great potential, instead being due to temporary physiological advantage. I call this phenomenon 'high performance blindness'. Most of the people entrusted with the task of spotting and developing talent are part of a totally colour-blind talent sect. They are only able to see a current, black-and-white snapshot of a player. Are they good, or not?

There is absolutely nothing wrong with a process of selection and rejection. That is in the nature of talent development. The problem is that when we are looking at children and young people, selection discriminates against more than 50 per cent of the talent mass. This is modern talent apartheid. Players born during the first few months of the year are often given opportunities that they have neither worked hard for nor deserve. They don't just get the best coaches and the best coaching; they also get more training, and self-confidence derived from the feeling that people believe in them. All this can give their motivation a powerful shove, making them more likely to put in the hours of training necessary to become really good.

No organisation and no country can afford to waste more than half the talent they have access to by staring blindly at what immediately meets the eye – an individual's current performance – and totally overlooking the story behind it in the process.

Performance blindness in business

This extreme waste of potential caused by poor talent identification is by no means only a sporting phenomenon. Many business executives and companies also suffer from high performance blindness. This often manifests itself in them becoming too obsessed with figures and results. Someone who has led a thriving business in an industry where the majority of companies are doing well, for instance, might appear to be a more attractive candidate for a high-level role than a similarly skilled or even better qualified candidate who has led a struggling firm in an industry in which most companies are failing.

In reality it is much more revealing to look at what people have accomplished *in the context in which they accomplished it* than than to look simply at results. This is why the best talent scouts in the world meticulously study the circumstances in which performances are created. In their splendid book, *The Talent Masters*, Ram Charan and Bill Conaty described how General Electric's charismatic chief executive, Jack Welch, would make a point of giving the highest-percentage bonus in the company to a manager who failed to hit their targets. This clearly makes the point that excellence is dependent ultimately on the circumstances in which it occurs – the chosen manager might have coped with a terrible business environment better than anyone else in the industry.

It's important, so let me say it again: don't judge potential using numbers alone. Dig below the surface to learn how the numbers were achieved or what stood in the way that might have prevented them from being better. As Charan and Conaty emphasise, a person could miss a target because the boss insisted that they retain a weak team member, or because the price of a critical resource suddenly spiked. Of course, all this is not to say that digging beneath the results is only important when somebody missed their targets. It's just as crucial when someone met the targets.

Was a manager successful more because of favourable market conditions rather than because they were a competent decision-maker? Did they sacrifice team members or long-term goals along the way to achieving their goals? Or was their success truly down to the fact that they excelled in all their responsibilities?

In order to know the right questions to ask, and in order to be able to answer them, you must have the courage and will to get up close to your people. There is no shortcut. Spotting talent that whispers is not something you can do from behind your desk in private. This is first and foremost because the process of spotting potential is defined far more by questions involving *why*, *when* and *how* than by questions about *what*.

As Stephen Francis puts it: 'I want to know their stories. I want to know what these people are all about and how they became who they are.'

2. Understand the difference between a fatal flaw and an opportunity

Consider this equation by Timothy Gallway, author of *The Inner Game of Tennis*:

Performance = potential – interference (P = p – i)

So performance is how well you actually do, potential is what you are truly capable of and interference refers to the factors that block the release of the potential. These come in all shapes and forms, including lack of knowledge, personal bias, a current bad leader, low confidence, lack of experience and so on.

In an ideal world, in which there were no interference, your performance would be *exactly* equal to your potential. What you see would be what you got. Such realities are rare, and high performance blindness means that executives, teachers and coaches often overlook unreleased potential. The key to getting better at spotting talent lies in eliminating or managing the interference.

Let's nip back to the Jamaican Gold Mine and the MVP Track and Field Club, where Stephen Francis explains how he spotted Shelly-Ann Fraser, the world and Olympic champion in the 100 metres:

'It was obvious to anyone that Usain Bolt had tremendous potential when he was sixteen. It was far more difficult to identify the potential possessed by Shelly-Ann Fraser, who was nineteen at that time. She took 11.7 seconds to run the 100 metres. She always ran well early in her races, but she fell apart technically and lost speed as the race went on. I thought, "Okay, if I can improve her technique and get her to train properly she will improve drastically." We succeeded in getting her right down to 10.73. Her example shows what it is I'm looking for. I'm looking for a weakness which I believe I can address and which can be decisive.'

Stephen Francis loves weaknesses – he sees them as opportunities for finding the rare talent that everyone else has overlooked. He is rigorous in identifying the interference factors that will accelerate or unblock a person's growth. After identifying them he asks himself two simple questions: can I eliminate the interference factor, and do I have the time to do it?

Everything he learns about newcomers is matched against his deeply held knowledge of what strengths are crucial for being a top sprinter – and what deficits don't matter. This approach requires that you refrain from seeing people as fully developed, pre-packaged products. It also requires that he as a coach understands the difference between a fatal flaw that will keep the person from advancing and a solvable issue that offers a real opportunity for development.

This principle is useful in any field. Let's try applying it in a business context, for example: looking at your team to find a member who, if a small problem with their work was addressed, would suddenly become much more valuable. Perhaps someone is really excellent in all the skills required to be promoted, indeed is better than many people already in that position, but is let down by a poor grasp of IT or finances. With a little training all that potential could suddenly be unlocked. Remember that if someone comes with problems, they also come with potential.

Great discoveries happen only if assessors are willing to suspend their idea of something perfect. Real potential does not necessarily look perfect, and it takes some open-mindedness, imagination and curiosity to identify talent that whispers.

3. Don't make your gate too narrow

One of the other major reasons that talent is overlooked is that our mental checklist of criteria is often very stereo-typed and narrow-minded. In almost any field you care to look at, the majority of 'prime' candidates tend to come from narrow channels and traditional backgrounds.

If you wanted to find a programmer you would probably think of searching a technical university, if you were looking for an executive you might think the best place to find them was a business college and if you wanted a teacher, then you'd likely interview people with the appropriate teaching certificates. These channels are well established and have operated with reasonable success for decades and decades. However, hunting just in those narrow and familiar zones won't find all the talent. When we narrow down our search excessively we risk overlooking a lot of impressive candidates.

As Stephen Francis says, 'There is no such thing as one kind of winning sprinter. World-class sprinters come in all sizes, and if I begin to narrow my mental model of what a winner looks like there is a big risk that I will overlook potential world record holders. The reward for keeping the gate as wide open as possible is the opportunity to sign a superstar that no-one else recognised.'

The world of sport is almost overflowing with examples of world-class athletes who did not fit the narrow, stereotypical models of what a winner looks like. Take the Swedish high jumper Stefan Holm, for example, who shook the world by winning the Olympic gold in Athens in 2004. What makes Holm particularly interesting is his height. He stands at 6ft (1.81m) which, although by no means short, is almost dwarf-like in the high jump. He regularly concedes six inches in height to his rivals, as well as being several inches shorter than the women's world number one, Blanka Vlasic of Croatia. Despite this, Holm boasts a personal best of 2.40 metres, and shares the unofficial world record of being able to clear the greatest height – 0.59cm – above his own height. If Stefan Holm had been judged by the usual height standards applied to high jumpers he would have been rejected almost before he started. And if someone had told Stefan Holm that he absolutely lacked the physical characteristics required to become one of the best in the world, he would probably not have been able to mobilise the self-belief necessary to even have a chance of winning. The point is that there is not one truth, one method, one technique, one type of winner. There are many, many ways to achieve the same goal.

Another good example of this is the Brazilian, Garrincha, who Pelé talks of as being the greatest Brazilian player ever, and the best dribbler in the history of football. Not only did Garrincha develop relatively late, he was born with crippled legs, with the left a full six centimetres shorter than the right. After being rejected by several teams because of his abnormal physique, he was finally taken on by the Brazilian club Botafogo. A player like Garrincha possesses none of the physical characteristics most people would believe a world-class footballer needs. Under a system like the ones that were used in the former Eastern Bloc and China – allocated players to the sport which best matched their physical profile – Garrincha, one of the best players the world has ever seen, would have been rejected on the spot, no doubt about it.

The cases of Holm and Garrincha show how important it is to keep an open mind and not to write people off on the basis of mechanistic tests and checklists, a practice that is becoming more and more rife in talent development the world over. Be sure that you don't fall prey to it – and that includes writing yourself off.

The exact same problem exists in the world of education. History is filled with story after story of famous people whose traditional education failed to help them identify their talent before they went on to brilliant careers. It turns out that about 35 per cent of all entrepreneurs in the US are dyslexic: Henry Ford, Richard C. Strauss, Charles Schwab, Walt Disney, John T. Chambers and Nelson Rockefeller, just to mention some of the most successful. And Virgin boss Richard Branson once recalled, 'They thought I was a hopeless case at school because I'm dyslexic, although no-one had heard of it in those days. I was always bottom of the class.'

Here we have people who performed poorly and were

labelled 'losers' in the established system, but who proved to possess enormous potential.

The Beatles show us two more classic cases of untapped talent. Paul McCartney went through his entire education without anyone noticing he had any musical talent whatsoever, as did George Harrison.

As Sir Ken Robinson, a leading thinker on education, creativity and innovation, put it: 'There was this one teacher in Liverpool in the '50s who had half the Beatles in his class and he missed it. I don't mean to say that you have to have failed at school before you can be a success, but an awful lot of people who did well after school didn't do well in school. And the point about this is that talent is often buried deep; it's not lying around on the surface. But our education systems at the moment are still very focused on a certain type of ability, and the result is that many very brilliant people are marginalised by the whole process.'

There are plenty of examples in any field of people who were originally tagged as 'unsuitable' because they didn't conform to some standard size, quality or look, but who nonetheless ended up performing extremely well later on. In his book *The Rare Find*, Georg Anders describes how in 2006, Facebook tried to break free of this pattern by launching a programming puzzle on its site, which later became known as the Puzzle Master. The puzzle was supposed to function as a test to find potential IT engineers and was so complicated that most people had great difficulty solving it.

Behind this idea was the assumption that there had to be masses of excellent IT engineers out there who had not found their way to Silicon Valley, and who had maybe got stuck in ordinary jobs elsewhere. The puzzle was an innovation designed to draw people like that out of the woodwork. Anyone could try their hand at it and send their solution to Facebook's head office in Palo Alto. The most successful 'applicants' would subsequently be called for interview.

It proved to be an extremely effective recruitment tool. By early 2011, Facebook had hired 118 people through Puzzle Master – almost 20 per cent of all its IT engineers. Many of them were college dropouts. Generally speaking, the puzzle seems to have offered a way to identify talent in people who had not trodden the traditional path, the kind of people who would almost certainly have failed miserably in a traditional company application procedure.

Facebook's Puzzle Master demonstrates the same principal as Stephen Francis and the MVP Track and Field Club: it proves that the world is full of overlooked talent. It is really worth challenging one's own stereotypes as to what talent looks like and spending time and energy looking in places where the competition does not look.

4. Put passion above skills

One of the most striking things about the MVP Track and Field Club in Kingston is the Spartan training facilities. You don't expect to see the world's best sprinters running and training on a grass field, but nonetheless, this is the situation at the MVP's training ground. The club provides the absolute basic necessities but no more. Nor does Stephen Francis have any plans to upgrade the facilities – in fact they are part of the way he tests new sprinters. Not by asking newcomers what they think of them directly; he watches their reactions. Are they interested in comfortable, impressive facilities, or are they simply driven by a deep-seated ambition to be one of the best in the world? As he puts it, 'The most important thing a man has to tell you is what he's not telling you.'

To Stephen Francis, the passion and hunger to be better today than you were yesterday is one of the most important indicators of the ability to succeed. He is not picking the fastest or strongest sprinters. He wants people with cunning and resilience, people who are able to bounce back from adversity. Once some basic level of competency is present, the key question stops being: what can you do today? Instead, it becomes: what can you learn today that will change your performance tomorrow? And what are you willing to do for it?

Stephen Francis says: 'I am not at all keen to use the word "talent", because in many people's minds this rarely involves hunger and hard work. Take, for instance, Brigitte Foster-Hylton [100 metres hurdles world champion]. When she came here as a 25 year old she ran the distance in 13.3. After the first year she ran it in 12.7. This convinced me that she could go all the way. She is in every way a role model when it comes to seriousness, single-mindedness and the attitude she brings with her to every training session.'

These are exactly the qualities that Angela Lee Duckworth, Assistant Professor of Psychology at the University of Pennsylvania, has noticed in her studies of successful teachers, sales people and students. People who accomplish great things, she found, usually combine a passion for a single mission with an unswerving dedication to achieve it, regardless of obstacles and the length of time it might take. Duckworth calls this quality 'grit' and has even developed a test to measure it, which she calls the Grit Scale. It is a deceptively simple test, in that it requires you to rate yourself in regard to twelve statements, from 'I finish whatever I begin' to 'I often set a goal but later choose to pursue a different one'. It takes only three minutes to complete, and it relies entirely on self-assessment, yet when Duckworth took it out into the field, she found it was a remarkably good predictor of success.

Grit is invisible on most resumes. It's hard to spot in a brief interview. Yet in profession after profession, it turns out to be the factor which decides who will exceed expectations and who will end up as a great disappointment.

A good story of how grit can manifest concerns Bob Gibbons, a former accountant, systems analyst, furniture executive and insurance salesman from North Carolina, who made his name as one of the most highly regarded college basketball recruiting analysts in the US during the early 1980s. In 1981 Gibbons was introduced to an eighteen-year-old boy from North Carolina. Although he had been ditched by the Laney High School basketball team, Gibbons felt there was something special about him. 'I saw a 6'3" player with explosive athletic ability,' Gibbons has since said. What impressed him most, however, was not the boy's performance on the basketball court; it was his attitude. After a high school tournament in North Carolina in 1981, he approached Gibbons after the match and introduced himself.

'Hello, Mr Gibbons. What did you think about my game today, and what can I do to improve?' he said.

The lad's name was Michael Jordan.

That season, Gibbons rated Jordan at 98 on a scale of 1–100, thus labelling him, in his opinion, the best high school player in the country. Most of the other scouts preferred players whose potential manifested itself in more black-and-white ways – those with very high scoring averages, for example. But Gibbons was convinced that the character traits he had seen in the young Michael Jordan were far more important than a high scoring average. History has certainly vindicated that view.

What characterises the world's best talent spotters is this ability to look into people's psyches and figure out how deeply they want to achieve something, and why. They have the courage to focus on a candidate's underlying character traits and motivations, rather than getting hung up on classic measures of ability. Not that performance, experience and the statistics that measure them are not important – but they are far from the whole show. When we get to know a person intimately, and understand their mindset, their hungers and their history, we can develop insights that will enable us to make an informed judgement about their true potential.

A final word about high potential scouting

It takes courage to look beneath the surface in this way. Had Stephen Francis not had the courage, Asafa Powell would probably never have surfaced. It means having the knowledge and foresight to select a tiny, pale strawberry which is not yet ripe rather than a juicy red one which will soon start to rot.

As Stephen Francis explains: 'If you want results right away, which is what most coaches aim for, or if you're under pressure, you will only see an athlete's performance.

It doesn't occur to you to delve behind that performance and find explanations for it. That is why people overlook the athletes with the greatest potential – because of lack of courage.'

We are often so afraid of making a mistake that we just play safe, to ensure that we at least do not make fools of ourselves. In this way, talent spotting becomes an attempt to avoid failure rather than an ambitious quest to find truly exceptional raw material.

Following the four scouting principles presented in this chapter will not guarantee that you make the right choice every time, but it will enable you to paint a much clearer picture of a person's potential. Even the very best talent spotters don't always get it right. In fact, they're struggling to get it right more than 50 per cent of the time. That's the way it will always be when you're trying to see something that doesn't actually exist yet. The whole thing is educated guesswork. What you're really trying to do is create an arbitrage. If you're right 25 per cent of the time versus rivals who are right 20 per cent of the time, you've created a 5 per cent arbitrage opportunity, and perhaps that 5 per cent will let you sprint ahead of the rest of the world, creating your very own MVP effect.

What you should never forget about TALENT IDENTIFICATION

1. The world is full of overlooked talent. Driving it to the surface requires that you rethink how and where you look. If you look in the same way and in the same places as everybody else, you'll get what everybody else gets.

2. Current performance can certainly be a strong indicator for potential, but that's far from always the case. Great potential does not necessarily manifest itself in current top performance.

3. Having a crystal clear understanding of the core competencies that drive success in a particular role will give you the freedom to look for and correctly identify relevant talent in many different places.

4. We typically hire for skills and fire for attitude. Start doing as Stephen Francis. Hire for attitude!

5. Shut up and start to listen! Talent identification is not about talking. It's about listening. Listen for the story, the theme and the reasons driving performance. Listen for what people say without saying it out loud. Listen for what you can't read in a resume.

Start early or
die soon

'Only one who devotes himself to a cause with his whole strength and soul can be a true master. For this reason mastery demands all of a person.'

Albert Einstein

In the world of football it's really all about the Brazilians. When you study FIFA's list of the world's best footballers since their Player of the Year award was first handed out in 1991, you will find that eight times out of twenty it has gone to a Brazilian. Now think about that. What are the chances of 40 per cent of the winners of a hugely prestigious award for the world's biggest, most popular sport coming from the same country? But impossible as it seems, this is what has happened. And Brazilian dominance does not stop there. In the 2010/11 Champions League, the world's finest club tournament, 79 Brazilians had time on the pitch, compared to only 25 Britains, 26 Germans and 49 Spaniards – and not a single Brazilian team takes part in the competition!

Over the last few years the mass exodus of football

players from Brazil has been huge. Since 1999 more than 1,000 Brazilian players each year have left their homeland to seek their footballing fortune, hoping for financial windfalls in Europe, Asia and the US, as well as in other South American leagues.

This apparently endless stream of excellent football players has been an irresistible bait for agents, coaches, journalists and scouts from all over the world. They have flocked to the Brazil in the hope of discovering the secret of this Gold Mine.

As usual, far-fetched explanations are rife. Special footballing genes, unique training methods, the natural joy of 'the beautiful game' and time spent playing football volley on Copacabana Beach are just a few of the ideas that have been laid on the table.

Europeans have assiduously attempted to mimic the 'Brazilian way'. Clubs have built beach pitches to replicate Copacabana. Samba rhythms have been introduced at training sessions. Players have been forced to kick a ball about barefoot just like the Brazilian boys in the favelas of São Paulo. Everybody wants to crack the code and discover how to create a new Ronaldo, Ronaldinho or Neymar, but so far without success. My own search for answers about Brazilian footballing excellence led me deep inside one of the favelas of Rio de Janeiro.

Guns, cool cash and football as a religion

Felipe nudges the ball with his foot as it rolls across the filthy street. He is one of twelve boys who have just organised a match in the middle of Rio's biggest favela, Rocinha. The houses around the pitch are built on top of each other like Lego bricks to accommodate the constantly rising population. Some 300,000 people currently live in Rocinha.

Felipe lopes about the asphalt pitch in a grimy jersey with 'Ronaldinho' printed on the back. He is only nine years old, but he already has an agent from Germany who pays for his shoes and his parents' rent and electricity bills. Of course, they want something in return, hoping that Felipe's footballing skills will one day land him a major contract. All the boys on the pitch in Rocinha have one thing in common: they know that their future depends on their abilities as footballers. No other opportunities exist. Even if they dream of becoming lawyers or businessmen, they know that in reality such dreams are unrealistic. Their families can hardly spare enough money to send them to one of the few, poor schools in the favela. So the boys play on the asphalt pitch in Rocinha every day.

Around the pitch, some shady looking people are gathered. A young man about twenty years old saunters round the edge of the asphalt with his son. Every now and then he turns away from the pitch, puts a small can to his nose and sniffs. It is glue. This is by no means a rare sight.

This, Rio's brutal dark side, is just twenty minutes' drive from the city's fashionable Ipanema neighbourhood and the beach at Copacabana with its rows of exquisite restaurants and affluent tourists lounging in deckchairs. In Rocinha the drug gang bosses have the last word in a lot of people's lives – they are involved in everything from issuing planning permission, to helping people settle their differences, to deciding what colour clothes people should wear. If a colour is associated with a rival gang, people are not allowed to wear it. In 1996 Michael Jackson had to seek the permission of the gangs to record his music video 'They Don't Care About Us' in the Santa Marta favela.

For young people with few, if any, opportunities, the gangs can offer a decent living. They can make up to 5,000 reais (£1,850) a month working for them. The gangs recruit members as young as ten years old. At that age they start by selling cocaine in small envelopes on the streets. The gangs prefer to use the really young kids to carry out the dirty work because they only have to serve short prison sentences. In the event of disputes between gangs or when fighting with the police breaks out it is not unusual to see teenagers walking the streets with AK-47s and grenades hanging off their belts. This is the world that will swallow Felipe and the other eleven children on the pitch unless their footballing skills can secure them a ticket out of there.

It is also not unusual for the best Brazilian footballers to have connections among the drug set. Flamengo superstar Vagner Love had some explaining to do recently when he was filmed on his way to a concert escorted by a crowd of drug dealers. And Adriano had to explain to the police how he had got his hands on a motorbike that was registered in the name of a drug dealer's mother. Other Brazilian top footballers have, over the years, dedicated some of their goals to gang bosses.

For the gangs, football represents a way of demonstrating their power. Once a year they hold the Coppa Rocinha, in which all the favela's teams play against one other. The matches are played with such intensity that one would think they were a question of life or death. On the sidelines, the drug dealers' talent spotters stand side-by-side with those from the big clubs like Flamengo, Cruzeiro and Fluminense, looking determinedly for potential material for their clubs. Felipe and the other boys on the pitch know that if they don't get discovered by the major teams there is good money to be earned playing for the gangs' teams. A contract with the Mafia pays 50 reais a match. One of Felipe's friends was recently offered a motorbike if he transferred to a gang's team.

I watch Felipe glide along the asphalt, hit the ball with the extreme tips of his toes and score. He clenches his fist. His team wins the day's match and the boys hug each other in jubilation.

More than 90 per cent of Brazil's top players grew up in poverty. In Brazil, football is the most obvious way for the people of the favelas to rise out of their difficult circumstances. While this escape route may be easy to visualise, it is also demanding. But Felipe knows that he has a chance – he sees the evidence upon the slopes of Rocinha where the great players from his district have built impressive homes for their families. These are daily reminders to all the boys of what they can become if they work hard enough.

The author playing with the boys in Favela Rocinha

Copacabana is overrated

'Forget Copacabana,' says the Godfather of Brazilian football, gesticulating at me with the fat brown cigar that is burning between his chubby fingers. 'When people come here to find out how we produce the world's best footballers the first place they go to is the beach at Copacabana. But they go there in vain. Copacabana is a myth.'

It is the day after my experience in the Favela Rocinha, and I am sitting face to face with 65-year-old Eurico Miranda. For ten years he was the president of Vasco da Gama, but he lost he position last year. That hurt. So much, in fact, that he has decided to take back the throne. And Eurico Miranda does not have a reputation for doing things by the book.

One of Brazil's major newspapers wrote of his entry into football politics: 'The other clubs' managers sat playing cards until Eurico Miranda kicked down the door, sat down at the table and started playing according to his own rules.'

It took me weeks to establish contact with Miranda. He is sick and tired of telling all and sundry about his football philosophy, he tells me, as we talk in his office in central Rio de Janeiro. But today he will make an exception, in spite of the fact that he is obviously not at all pleased that I am wearing shorts in his office.

'Our top players are not hatched on Copacabana or Ipanema,' he says. '95 per cent of them have been created on the street corners of the favelas. Just think how many times a Brazilian boy playing for hours on end every day in the street touches the ball. That is the kind of head start that you can't catch up with. The biggest mistake they make in Europe is being too well organised. Brazilian footballers are not a product of organised talent development. The secret is spontaneous, unorganised football. Our academies do not do anything different or better than those anywhere else. They just have to make sure not to ruin the raw material they take in. The work has already been done for them.'

Just pick them up in the streets

When I study the great Brazilian players in depth, it turns out that Miranda is perfectly right. It's the same story with many of the Brazilian players – Pelé, Ronaldinho, Robinho, Ronaldo, Zico and all the others grew up in poverty playing on the streets every day. Very little of their training was done in clubs. They practised on their own. In fact, Brazilian talent development was not systematised until five years ago, when the first academies along the lines of those in Europe began to be set up. In other words, the top players we see today in the major international football arenas were not trained in an established system; they are the direct products of unorganised football on the streets.

I get exactly the same impression when I fly into Congonhas Airport in São Paulo a couple of days later, landing amid the enormous skyscrapers of this vast metropolis. With a population of twenty million, São Paulo is the world's fifth-largest city. The chaos here makes a traffic jam in New York seem like a trivial misunderstanding on a quiet residential street.

I'm here to visit the football academy established by the supermarket chain Pão de Açúcar. The training ground consists of three pitches and an office block juxtaposed between giant hotels, motorway bridges and slum districts.

Pão de Açúcar Football Academy is located in downtown São Paulo

As I arrive at the ground the Academy's under-seventeen team is getting ready for the weekend match. Behind one of the goals stands the academy's director, Thiago Mendes, keeping an eye on them.

'A fifteen-year-old European boy knows that if he can't make a go out of football, his country will take care of him,' he says. 'That's not the way it is here. You either earn millions playing football or you end up with nothing. Most of our players come from the favela, where they often have four or five siblings they have to provide for. Football is their only chance.'

Three years after opening, Sendas Pão de Açúcar is a tremendous success. The academy has already produced several national youth team players and sent a good number of them off to top clubs in Europe. But according to Thiago Mendes, the academy itself cannot really take credit for this success.

'In reality, all we have to do is go out onto the street and pick them up. No Brazilian club needs to worry about what they have been doing up to the age of thirteen or whether they have put in the necessary hours of training.

It is our streets that develop our players. If we didn't have players with that level of skill at thirteen years old then we would have nothing,' Thiago tells me.

The deeper I delved into the world of Brazilian football, the more apparent it became to me that their mass production of top players has very little to do with the quality of the country's organised talent development. It is down to the fact that most boys in this country of 200 million people play football, gaining an extreme number of training hours early in their lives playing on the streets. And for most of them there really isn't any alternative – becoming a good footballer is their only route out of a life of poverty.

This creates a recruitment base not seen anywhere else in the world. Even grade B Brazilian players are top notch. Take, for instance, the major club Cruzeiro which rejects 4,000 players under the age of fifteen for every one which it takes in. Carry that figure forward to the under-twenties, where the competition is even fiercer, and you get one in 126,000. To give some point of comparison, Sweden scarcely even has that many players. As Thiago Mendes explains: 'Nowhere else in the world do we find so many boys with that many hours of training under their skin at such an early juncture in their lives.'

Although at times it may seem that Ronaldinho and Neymar fell from heaven as blessings to 'the beautiful game', the truth is much simpler. The many millions of times they touched the ball throughout their childhood on the streets prepared them to do what we see them do on the pitch today. The Brazilian football empire therefore invites us to consider the following question: when we think we see God-given talent, are we not in fact simply seeing people who have consciously or unconsciously trained a hell of a lot at an early age?

The expert on experts

Interestingly enough, this theory enjoys huge support in the scientific world, which over the last 30 years has intensified its quest to understand high performance. Anders Ericsson, a Professor of Psychology at Florida State University, is the expert on experts. He has spent the last 30 years interviewing and analysing high-flying experts in all kinds of fields, from gymnasts to chess players to violinists.

In the 1990s Ericsson and a group of scientists carried out a study at an academy for elite musicians in West Berlin. Their results would prove to challenge the most fundamental conceptions of what leads to elite performances. The academy lay in what was then West Berlin and had a reputation for producing some of the world's very best musicians. The vast majority of its students later joined the world's most reputable symphony orchestras or became soloists on the international stage. With the help of the academy's lecturers and professors, Ericsson and his colleagues divided the institution's violinists into three groups. Group one consisted of the stars who were expected to become world-class soloists. Group two consisted of first rate and promising violinists who were not quite of the same standard as those in group one. Group three consisted of those violinists who were not expected to join the world elite, but who were likely to make a living from music, for example as school and college teachers. To be specific, Dr Ericsson's mission was to clarify the reasons for the different standards of the three groups. Why had some become better than others?

It turned out that all the violinists had started playing their instrument at more or less the same age, around eight years old. They typically decided to go all out and pursue a career as a musician seven years later, at the age of fifteen. All of them also had the exact same teachers and they received the same amount of scheduled instruction during the week at the academy. In other words, everything pointed to the fact that it must have been raw talent that made the violinists in group one better than those in group three.

As part of the study the students were asked to decide which activity had been the most decisive in improving them as violinists. All agreed that self-training was the most effective activity; the practice they did on their own. What is more, not only did they agree that it was the most efficient form of training, they also said it was the most mentally demanding, and far from enjoyable.

The interesting thing was that while the students understood the importance of this kind of practice and had the time to do it, not all of them spent a lot of time doing it. Group one and group two each studied for about 24 hours a week on their own, but members of group three studied for only about nine hours. Simple arithmetic shows a difference of 780 hours a year in the time spent practising.

All this provides a convincing explanation as to why groups one and two were more competent than group three. It does not, however, explain why group one was superior to group two. If the number of hours spent practising is the critical factor when it comes to being a first-rate player, why do we not find the stars in group one practising more than the merely promising violinists of group two?

Ericsson and his team answered this question by taking

an in-depth look at the students' training histories. On top of assessing the number of hours they currently put in, all of them had been asked to estimate the amount of time they had spent per week year-on-year since they had first picked up a violin. When the researchers compared these figures, everything became clear. As eighteen year olds, the violinists in group one had spent an average of 7,410 hours of their lives practising; group two had spent an average of 5,302 hours; and group three had only practised for 3,420 hours. In other words, students in group one had worked much, much harder than students in groups two and three.

The study of the Berlin violinists shocked the music world, which seems to have quite a deep-seated belief in the idea of innate talent. It seems an obvious explanation for why some people are tone deaf while others play so well that your hair stands on end. In fact, Ericsson and his team did not find any violinists who were among the best but who did not put in the same amount of practice as the others – nobody was that talented. It is equally interesting to note that neither were there any violinists who had put in the hours of training generally required but who had failed to rise to the level one would therefore expect.

As Ericsson puts it: 'When a musician has reached a standard high enough for him or her to be admitted to an elite academy [again: you just have to be "good enough"], the number of hours they currently spend practising and have spent practising in the past are the critical factor which separates the best from the second best and the second best from the rest. Nothing else.'

In other words, high performance seems first and foremost to be a choice that you can make – as long as you are willing to invest what it takes.

Two hours and forty-four minutes every day
for ten years

The deeper researchers on high performance have delved into the history of so-called elite performers, the more they agree that their journey to success is rarely, if ever, a short sprint and is usually an exacting marathon. There is even some consensus on the amount of training required to become world class: 10,000 hours. Ten thousand hours of training is equivalent to putting in two hours and forty-four minutes *every day* for ten years. This gave rise to the so-called Ten Years Rule, which has been very succinctly expressed by Nobel Prize winner Herbert Simon: 'Becoming world-class in any domain, from mathematics to violin to chess, requires ten years of committed training.'

Or in the words of neurologist Daniel Levitin: 'In study after study of composers, basketball players, authors, skaters, pianists, chess players and even criminals (if they are not caught and jailed too often), the 10,000 hours turn up time and time again.'

So there is no doubt that you must pool at least a decade of focused training to truly master anything. In a 1985 study of 120 elite athletes, artists, biochemists and mathematicians, every single top performer invested a minimum of ten years' training to achieve international recognition in their field. Olympic swimmers and the best pianists actually trained an average of fifteen years before attaining the highest level. The ten-year rule is a very rough estimate of what it takes to achieve international class; most researchers regard it as a minimum. In music and literature, for example, elite performers often do not reach the pinnacle of their careers for twenty or thirty years. There are no shortcuts. As Bob Bowman, coach of the American swimming legend Michael Phelps, once said: 'Michael has not taken a single day off in five years. He even trained on Christmas Eve and on his birthday.'

When people who are leaders in their fields are asked about the secret of their success, it is very rare indeed to hear them say: 'I was just better than the others, I was more talented.' They are far more likely to say that they focused more, made greater sacrifices, worked harder and were more passionate about what they did. It seems that anyone who thinks that talent means that success will come quickly or easily is setting themselves up to be disappointed. As Anders Ericsson explained to me: 'When we look at the people we like to call talented, it would appear that they do not have to work particularly hard to succeed. They make everything look so easy. But the opposite is actually the case. Almost invariably the best performers are those who train the most. I have yet to meet someone who did not earn their success through hard work and thousands of hours of training.'

Six-year-old girls and their hitting partners

So the explanation of the success of Brazilian players is far simpler than we tend to think. Let's jump back to young Felipe in Favela Rocinha. Having had a kick about and a chat with the Felipe and the other lads, I punched the number of hours they train every week into my pocket calculator. When I multiplied all their weekly training hours in school, the club and on the street together, I found that they put in 22 weekly training hours. If a nine-year-old Brazilian boy has trained for 22 hours a week since the age of five, he will have accumulated 4,576 hours of training. If he continues at this rate he will have reached the magic 10,000 hours by age thirteen! Just like the musicians in Ericsson's study, the Brazilian boys did most of their training on their own. The fact that this self-training is so crucial raises the question of what really matters in the performance of a teacher, coach or manager. Is it what they make their charges do while they are with them, or is it rather what they can inspire them to do when they are not?

The 10,000 hours seem to be inescapable. It seems that when we are convinced that we see raw, innate talent, we are in reality simply seeing 10,000 hours of training consumed at a very early stage in a person's life.

Brazil is a huge country, with a population in excess of 200 million, where virtually every boy plays football, where there is a football pitch on the first floor of most condominiums and where it is by no means unusual for a boy to have played 10,000 hours before his thirteenth birthday.

It seems clear enough that this is the reason that Brazilians have scooped half the awards for the best footballer in the world since 1993. And this correlation of training hours with success is also borne out by the other five Gold Mines.

We have yet to explore the Russian tennis Gold Mine in depth but there it is by no means unusual for six-year-old girls to have hitting partners and their own personal physiotherapists. Not only do the Russian girls start training far earlier than, for instance, their American counterparts, but they also do so for different reasons. At Spartak Tennis Club in Moscow, children's coach Elena Kosiskya explained to me: 'We start training them five times a week from the age of five here. In the United States they start to do that when the children are nine or ten, and for the first few years they only play for fun. Here, we train them to be champions from day one.'

A Russian girl training at Spartak Tennis Club in Moscow

Little girls in Moscow getting clear instructions

More or less the same pattern manifested itself in South Korea, where it is not unusual for South Korean junior golfers to train three times as much as American juniors. As one of the coaches, Won Park, said to me as we sat at the driving range in Seoul: 'We have a rule here: you train from sunup to sundown and then you do physical training.'

Morning training at a driving range in Seoul

The latest hit in South Korea is virtual golf. The country now has more than 3,000 golf cafes and more than

12,000 golf simulators, most of them in Seoul. Players can check in at any time of the day with their own golf clubs for a virtual round on the world's most distinguished courses. Young South Koreans frequent golf cafes like Americans go to Starbucks. I arrived at my hotel in Seoul at around midnight and business executives were still honing their skills at the hotel's indoor driving range down in the basement.

Still running with his school books

The Ethiopian Gold Mine is Bekoji. Despite having a population of only 30,000 people it spits out one long-distance running world champion after another. Yet again people here seem to hit the target of 10,000 training hours early on. The infrastructure in Bekoji is poor, to put it mildly. The town is five hours by car from the capital Addis Ababa, the last three hours along deeply pitted dirt roads. Because of this, only two of the town's 30,000 inhabitants have cars.

The preferred means of transport here is 'Shanks's pony' – walking, or rather running. Old people walk or run 20 km to market and 20 km back again every week. Many children run as far as 10 km to school and 10 km home again. Added to this is the fact that Bekoji lies 3,000 metres above sea level, meaning that simply by living there the population produces masses of red blood cells, which are vital to long-distance runners. They live slap bang in the middle of perfect conditions and so benefit from this natural form of blood doping. One could say that Bekoji boys and girls train to be super athletes without even being aware of it. They certainly achieve 10,000 hours of training time at a very early stage in their lives, and under these highly beneficial conditions.

The entrance to the only running track in Bekoji

Boys of Bekoji training from 6 a.m.

On my last day in Ethiopia I meet the legendary Haile Gebrselassie. With eight World Championships under his belt, two Olympic gold medals and more than 25 world records, his CV speaks for itself. Haile is in many respects the perfect example of the substance of the Ethiopian superstars. He was born in the town of Assella, 50 km from Bekoji, where he grew up in poverty on a farm and, like many other children, had to run 10 km to school every morning and 10 km home again every evening.

'Running 10 km to school every day at high altitude turned out to be the perfect preparation for my career,' he tells me.

It also gave Gebrselassie a very special running style. He always runs with his left arm slightly bent. There's a very simple reason for this: he used his arm to carry his books on the way to school. Over time, it simply became part of his running style. Even today, Haile Gebrselassie runs as though he is still carrying his school books.

'This hand is not always very active,' he says, looking down at his right arm. 'I used to carry my books in the other hand. My carrying hand was always my strongest.'

The author meeting Haile Gebrselassie in Addis Ababa

It's a similar story among the Kenyan runners. Many began their running careers as early as four or five years old, looking after the family's goats. If they came home and there was a goat missing they were in serious trouble, so they were constantly vigilant, and didn't mind running around the hills to keep tabs on the herd. Many of them also ran to and from school.

As Moses Kiptanui puts it: 'We ran to school to avoid a

caning for being late. We were actually training to become athletes without realising it. The teacher didn't realise, either, that she was actually training us by punishing us when we turned up late.'

Of course, all this is not to say that all people have equal potential, and that everybody could become a world-class runner. Haile Gebrselassie and Moses Kiptanui, even if they hadn't spent countless hours running to school in high altitude, would probably still have been good runners. But without those hours to school, they would never have reached the heights of achievement which they have.

The huge amount of training that East Africans get under their belts at a very early age, consciously or unconsciously, gives them a foundation which no-one in the Western world can match. As one of the best American marathon runners of all time, Alberto Salazar has said: 'In Kenya there are maybe 1 million schoolboys who run 16–20 kilometres a day. An eighteen-year-old Kenyan runner will have run about 25,000 to 30,000 kilometres further in his life than your average American boy.'

It is interesting to think what might happen if you took ten American girls and boys aged eight to live in Kenya, in Iten's running environment. Would they also develop into some of the world's best middle- and long-distance runners? Or could a British invasion of the rostra at the 2016 Olympics be achieved if you took a group of English children, put them up with host families in the Pyrenees and got them to run between 80 and 110 kilometres every week for the next seven years?

There is no way an experiment like this would ever be carried out, of course, but as a thought experiment it helps us to challenge our convictions about what it is that creates world class.

Early starters stay ahead of the rest

Let us return to the roots of this discussion: the Brazilian favelas, where the foundations for great accomplishments in the world's football arenas are laid. Take a look at the training curve of Felipe from Rocinha (the solid line) who, just like many other Brazilian boys, will achieve his 10,000 hours at the age of thirteen.

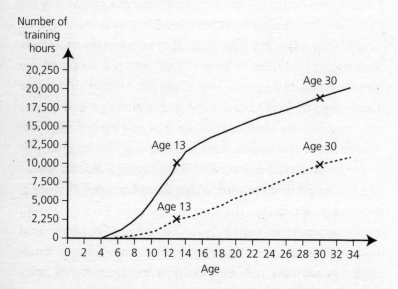

This is in glaring contrast to an English lad (the dotted line) who maybe also starts when he's five but who only trains for a couple of hours three times a week. Following a programme like that, at the age of thirteen he will only have trained for 2,544 hours, and if he continues at that rate it will take him until the age of 30 to reach 10,000 hours. If, at the age of fifteen, he is good enough to get into an English football academy – where they train four or five times a week – he will achieve his 10,000 hours a few years earlier. However, it is probably already too late to catch up with a Brazilian boy.

So there is a lot to indicate that early training is vital for success. They are aware of this in South Korea. Indeed, some parents are so concerned about making sure their children train enough that they take their children out of school, sometimes as early as at the age of ten. As Won Park explains: 'If you reach the age of 25 and have not yet won a significant tournament you are a catastrophe. You must start early if you are to get anywhere.'

This does not only apply to the world of sport. Think back to the violinists in Berlin. The only reason people in group one (7,410 hours of training) were better than those in group two (5,302 hours) and group three (3,420 hours) was that they had worked harder. Far, far harder. Not just today or yesterday, either, but since they were seven years old.

A young violinist in group three might decide to aim to join the world violinist elite at age eighteen. Unfortunately, the brutal fact is that the best violinists in his age group, those he needs to match, have already spent more than twice the number of hours practising than him. To catch up, he would have to spend many, many more hours practising than his counterparts.

And if he is in group three (spending about nine hours a week in practice) then he would have to more than double his current hours simply to match the training schedules of the group one students (about 24 hours a week), let alone go beyond them. In other words, the late starter would be a pensioner before he had the necessary amount of training

THE GOLD MINE EFFECT

under his belt. Although in theory it would be possible for someone in this position to practise their way into the world's violinist elite, in reality it would not be achievable.

Windows of opportunities

The hours of practice early starters put in are not just valuable in themselves – they also physically and mentally prepare them for the many subsequent hours they will need to spend in order to truly excel. In Bekoji and Iten, for example, the kids who run everywhere in their bare feet are unconsciously building up their motor apparatus, which will enable them to cope with large amounts of training later in life. They are training in order to be able to train even more.

The view that early training carries benefits beyond merely helping a person to reach the magic 10,000 hours at an earlier age is backed up by research. Psychologists and neurologists speak of there being particular windows of opportunity in our development – specific phases, during which training is decisive if one is to remain in the running as a potential world-class performer in a given field. If you do not learn the necessary skills during that period, the window closes and you lose the chance of being among the very best.

Michael Jordan learned this the hard way. After he left basketball as the greatest player of all time, he tried to repeat the trick in baseball. He signed a contract with the Chicago White Sox. However, he was as great a failure in baseball as he was a success in basketball. He got nowhere near playing in the best American league. But why? Here was one of the world's very best athletes, a genuine winner, totally committed to succeeding in his new sport. But despite his extreme training efforts he ended up failing to make a mark.

In his book *Why Michael Couldn't Hit*, neurologist Harold Klawans presents his theory of what went wrong. One of the main reasons, as he saw it, was that Michael Jordan was way past his window of opportunity. Being among the best hitters in baseball requires outstanding hand-eye coordination and body-balance control. These relatively complex skills require early specialisation. It is reasonable to assume that if there's a twelve year old you have not trained adequately to receive and hit the ball shooting towards you, you can forget all about joining the world elite. No matter how good you are at basketball.

People can always improve, though not always to the highest level. According to Harold Klawans, if you do not start training in a particular discipline until you are twenty, it will be impossible to programme the brain with the required skills to the required level, and you will never be able to catch up with those who started ten years earlier. Hence Michael Jordan's attempt at a second sporting career was always doomed to failure.

Dr Anthony Kalinowski, a researcher at the University of Chicago, made another important finding relating to early specialisation. Kalinowski discovered that on average, American swimmers who make the national championships will have started training at age ten. In comparison, those selected for the United States Olympic team started training at an average of seven years old. Similarly, the best violinists of the 20th century – all of whom had international careers as soloists spanning over 30 years – were found to have begun practising their instrument at an average age of five, while violinists of merely national prominence started at eight. Getting a head start really makes a difference.

Why you should start early

So precisely how early can and should you start training if you want to become world class in your field? And when is it too late? The answers to those questions depend largely on three parameters.

1. Competitive pressures in the discipline

The effort required to achieve world-class performance depends on the level of competition in the particular discipline. If you want to reach the top in curling, you can probably do so with significantly less than 10,000 hours of training and also get away with starting out later in life. If you want to make it big in football, in which the physical demands are higher and competition much more intense, it's a different story. Show me a footballer who has played in the Champions League and got there with fewer than 10,000 hours of training – in most cases it will be a lot more than that. Likewise, show me a basketball player in the American NBA who has trained for less than 15,000 hours, a top South Korean golfer on the LPGA tour who has trained less than 20,000 hours.

There are none, and if you can find any I will gladly run naked from Iten in Kenya to Bekoji in Ethiopia. My travels and research in the six Gold Mines showed that if you want to become world class in sports like tennis, golf, football and athletics, you are more likely to need 20,000 hours of training than 10,000 – the competition is that fierce.

In Japan, children trained in gymnastics for up to twelve hours a day in order to prepare for the London Olympics in 2012. Working at that rate means you can hit 10,000 hours in only a little over two and a half years.

The lesson here is simple: your own speed means nothing if other people are running faster. It's no good having 10,000 training hours in your knapsack if your competitors have 20,000, and this is where the rule comes unstuck. What it takes to achieve world class in a specific field is a dynamic concept and changes over time. As records are broken, the bar is raised when it comes to the number of hours of training you need to consume to become world class.

The same principle counts in business. How much effort and how many hours you are going to have to practise to become the best are defined by your market. In many markets, it takes 10,000 hours of preparation to win because *most people give up after 5,000 hours.* In other markets where the rewards for succeeding are huge and the competition ruthless, the number is probably closer to 20,000 hours or more. For endeavours like being CEO of a Fortune 500 company or partner in a worldwide consultant firm, 10,000 hours might not be enough.

2. The complexity of the discipline

The more complex the skills you have to master, the more crucial early practice is. One example is gymnastics, which is extremely physically complex, requiring highly developed balance, coordination, muscle-control and so on. If you do not start specialising as a seven or eight year old you will never make the world elite. Your 'window of opportunity' will have closed.

In contrast, take long-distance running, which in purely technical terms is not nearly as complex. In this discipline you could get away with specialising much later than age seven and still manage to become world class. The three-times steeplechase World Champion Moses Kiptanui may well have run as a child, but it was not until age eighteen that he began to train consciously and seriously in order to join the world elite.

An interesting pattern emerges when you study the British medal haul from the 2008 Beijing Olympics. British athletes brought home a total of 119 gold medals, which is surely an acceptable performance for a nation with a population of 60 million. It was only bettered by the major powers – China, the United States and Russia. The interesting thing, though, is that the gold medals were won across very few disciplines. Cycling, canoeing/kayaking, rowing and sailing are particularly prominent in the statistics and account for almost 90 per cent of all the British gold medals.

These sports are known as 'big engine sports'. That is, they do require a lot of strength and stamina but are relatively simple in their technical demands. In theory, you could take a world-class rower and transform him within a few years into a world-class cyclist. The critical factors required for success in both disciplines are similar to, and overlap, each other.

Take, for example, Eric Heiden, the American speed-skater who won five Olympic golds. After his speed-skating career, Heiden became a professional cyclist, and went on to win the American championships and complete the Giro d'Italia. Because of its relatively low technical complexity, cycling is not a sport in which you have to specialise at an early age, so Heiden was able to transfer his physical capacities from speed-skating directly to cycling and quickly achieve results. Another example is the Cuban Alberto Juantorena. Originally a basketball player, he became an Olympic 400- and 800-metre running champion later in life. This kind of transition can only successfully be made to a sport which does not require early specialisation. There is no way Juantorina would have succeeded if he had taken the plunge into gymnastics, skating, table tennis or baseball, all of which demand far earlier specialisation than middle-distance running. Remember the lesson of Michael Jordan.

This all tells us the reason that Britain does not win medals in gymnastics, taekwondo, tennis and table tennis: the Brits simply do not train early enough in some disciplines, meaning their windows of opportunity have already closed.

3. The point at which you must peak

The earlier you need to peak in your discipline, the more important it is to specialise early. This applies in gymnastics, in which girls typically peak between the ages of thirteen and sixteen. If they are to train in gymnastics for 10,000 hours before they reach that age, they must specialise as four or five year olds. The best female gymnasts at the 2012 Olympics will have been born around 1995. Generally speaking, girls have to specialise earlier than boys, simply because they develop earlier and therefore have fewer years at their disposal before their window of opportunity closes.

The same principle applies in football, where players are peaking earlier and earlier. If you have not acquired the basic technical skills of football by the time you are twelve you can forget all about playing international football professionally. Golf, on the other hand, is a sport in which many people peak relatively late, meaning that it is not absolutely necessary to start before you are ten.

It is also important to understand that early specialisation and many hours of training early in life are far more decisive factors in sport than they are, for example, in commerce or the arts. This is primarily due to physical factors, which in sport naturally impose limits on the length of an athlete's career.

Nothing else to do

I understand that all these calculations of what you need to do to become the best in the world at something may sound cold and cynical. The fact is, however, that you really do have to be this single-minded and focused on your goal. You have to make sacrifices.

But here is something else to think about: not everyone has to aim to be the best in the world. To make significant, even life-changing progress in a particular area (to advance professionally, for example), you most likely don't have to devote yourself to your goal with the single-minded ferocity that is required to become world class. However, understanding the features in common which allowed Ronaldinho, Haile Gebrselassie or the Berlin violinists to become the world's best will very likely show you how to get better at what you do as well.

And the evidence is clear: training is not what you do when you've got where you're going. It is what gets you there. *Whether you are a mathematician, a footballer, a business executive or run a sandwich bar, if something extraordinary is to come out, then something extraordinary must go in.* Large quantities of practice hours make you good. Exceptionally large quantities make you excellent, perhaps even world class.

It is very unlikely many world stars sit down and calculate how much time they need to train and how early they need to start in order to be among the very best. Their beginnings are often much more arbitrary than that. For example, we often underrate the fact that people simply become good because there is nothing else to do where they live. Remember Bekoji in Ethiopia – people there become good runners because there is simply nothing else to do.

Before I went to Bekoji, Richard Nerirkar, the former British elite runner and director of the Great Ethiopian Run, told me this: 'You can't do anything there. You can't earn any money, you can't get a good education and you can't really build a business. Running gives people in Bekoji meaning and purpose.'

We've already seen that the same thing is true in Brazil, where the dearth of choice drives millions of Brazilian boys into intensive football training very early in life. Or we could point to Tärnaby, a village in north-west Sweden with a miniscule population of 533 which, over the years, has produced some of the world's best skiers – Anja Pärson, Stig Strand and the legendary Ingemar Stenmark are but a few of them. The village lies isolated in the snow-covered Swedish wilderness and choices there are limited, to put it mildly. In other words, the optimum conditions exist for children to put in an extreme number of skiing hours early in life. Life in Tärnaby is certainly far less brutal than in

Rocinha, but just like in the Brazilian favela, the buffet consists of very few dishes.

This is in stark contrast to most of the Western world, where people have enormous freedom and are given all kinds of opportunities. But if you want to be good at something, is having so much choice a good thing? How can you possibly achieve your 10,000 hours of training early enough if you grow up in an El Dorado of choices, all of them open to you and between which you can surf at leisure?

The Paradox of Choice

We typically prize having choices; we usually want to have as many as possible. We see autonomy and freedom of choice as critical to our well-being. However, though people in the West today have more choice than any group have had in history (and thus, presumably, more freedom and autonomy), they don't necessarily benefit from it. Too much choice can be a bad thing, causing decision paralysis and unhappiness. This phenomenon is widely known as the Paradox of Choice.

In 2000 two American psychologists, Dr Sheena S. Iyengar and Dr Mark R. Lepper, set up a tasting booth at an upmarket grocery store in California. Each day they set out a selection of jams; some days there would be six types, other days there would be 24. Although the wider selection attracted more shoppers, more people actually bought the jam when faced with the narrower range. The more choices people had, the harder it was for them to make a decision.

This is generally true of modern life – we are bombarded with an endless stream of mundane little decisions.

We stand in the breakfast cereal aisle of the supermarket and are confronted with shelf after shelf of different ways to eat corn and wheat, stretching away as far as the eye can see. The internet gives us access to news, games, television, Facebook and a million other ways to pass our time. Young men and women are increasingly reluctant to make the ultimate commitment and get married, and that is likely due at least in part to all the other glittery options competing for their attention: friends, professional success, the media and all the people in the world they haven't yet dated. Our grandparents had a couple of TV channels to choose between, we now have 850. It's impossible not to constantly wonder if there's something better, or someone better.

The reason that this causes anxiety for many people is that choice always involves a loss. When you choose one direction, you lose the opportunity of going in another. Economists use the term 'opportunity costs' to describe the things a person misses out on when they choose one thing over another. Thus the more options we are faced with, the more opportunity costs we have to accept, and the more unhappy and restless we potentially become. Sometimes we simply freeze and check-out, not choosing anything at all in order to avoid dealing with the opportunity costs of our decisions. We get stuck at the jam table of life, wanting to choose something but unwilling to shut any other choices out. This doesn't just happen when people are shopping; it happens when we're doing much more important things, such as choosing our career path.

There is an old saying, 'If you want to take the island, then burn your boats,' meaning that if you totally commit to something, giving yourself no way to go back, you are more likely to succeed. For the modern person, making that kind of commitment is harder than ever before.

Why not start early?

Since we live in a world of intense, global competition, anyone who wants to develop their talent in any sphere, be it sports, business, the arts or education, must constantly improve him or herself. If training – and preferably lots of it – is the most decisive factor when it comes to improving oneself, then shouldn't we try harder to inspire children to pursue their passions and interests in a more dedicated way, and as young as possible? Or, if they have not yet found a passion, perhaps we should train them to do something so well that they will naturally develop an enthusiasm for it. In the words of Haile Gebrselassie: 'I started running to school because I couldn't afford a bike. I realised I was fast, so running became my way out of poverty, and then suddenly, I started loving it. I realised that I could help other people by running fast and that it was a great way of learning what you can achieve if you really want.'

Ideally you want young people to take responsibility for their own training as young as possible. You want them to start reaching beyond the programme they are given, addressing their development needs on their own. But how do you get them to that point quickly as? This is what Marjie Elferink-Gemser, a Dutch professor of sports science, has called 'early ownership'. If we stop worrying about early training and commit to it then we give ourselves the chance to create a framework in which it is possible to achieve the necessary 10,000 hours quickly while still allowing the child's personality to develop at the same time.

Why not abandon the illusion that a child needs to do a little of everything – yoga on Wednesdays and French on Thursdays – for them to be 'complete'? Why not accept that top performance requires a very one-dimensional focus but that a child can easily have a good life and feel at ease with what they have *not* chosen as well as what they have? Theoretically, if you start training a child in business and finance from the age of five (which they are unlikely to enjoy), by the time they reach the age of 25 you could have them operating at the standard of another executive twice their age. Yes, I am perfectly aware that most people believe that you can only be really great at something if you love it. I don't agree with that. Love can certainly help, as it will make you more likely to spend time training, but many people still stink at the things they love. Loving something doesn't mean you'll be great at it.

The main reason that people find this lesson hard to digest is that they really want to believe effort is a myth. They would prefer to think that in-born talent is the key to success. But effort really is crucial. As the American marketing expert Seth Godin puts it: 'Effort takes many forms. Showing up. Taking risks. Getting rejected. Investing yourself. Being kind when it's more fun not to. Paying forward when there's no hope of tangible reward. Doing the right thing.'

But again, it's easier to bet on luck. That's why diet books that simply say, 'eat less, exercise more' maybe don't sell many copies, as good as that advice may be. Effort is really a choice. Being world class often demands a great deal of effort in an early age, the option of improvement is completely available to everyone. All the time.

What you should never forget about PRACTICE

1. Practice is the mother of all world-class performance. When you think you see god-given talent in a business leader, a musician or an athlete, what you really see is likely to be somebody who consciously or unconsciously got 10,000 hours of practice in at an early age.

2. Just because you love doing something, doesn't necessarily mean you will ever be great at doing it. The greatest payback often comes when you least want to carry on.

3. World-class performance requires that people start practising at an early age; just how early depends on the discipline. The more complex the skill set you need to master, the earlier you must start. However, improvement is available for everyone.

We're all quitters

'Mind is everything: muscles – pieces of rubber. All that I am,
I am because of my mind.'

Paavo Nurmi, one of only four athletes ever to win
nine Olympic gold medals

It is 3 July 1991 at the Olympic Stadium in Stockholm, and a new chapter in the history of athletics is being written. Five hundred metres into the 3,000-metre steeplechase, a black runner effortlessly pulls ahead of the rest of the field. Nobody can keep up with him. And the strange thing is that he doesn't even have a number on his back. He is an entirely unknown quantity, and yet 400 metres before the finish it looks like he's set to break the world record.

'Who is this?' asks an astounded announcer.

A few minutes after the runner has crossed the line as the winner, the Swedish organisers announce that his name is Moses Kiptanui.

The day before he had been on a plane from Nairobi to Stockholm with his agent, a British journalist by the name of Kim McDonald. Moses had actually joined the Kenyan army and was living on a military base in Nyahururu in western Kenya, but was suddenly given the opportunity to come to Europe and compete. On the plane Kim McDonald told Kiptanui that he couldn't guarantee him a place in an event, but that he hoped to get into the 1,500 metres at the last moment. Out of eagerness to get into a race, Moses suggested to his agent that he could run in the 3,000-metre steeplechase if necessary. He had won a couple of races in the discipline back home at the military base and believed he could do the same in Europe.

When they arrived in Stockholm it turned out that there were indeed no places in the 1,500 metres, but Moses have the last vacant place in the steeplechase. Because of his last-minute arrival neither the media nor the result service was informed about the new Kenyan runner. That's why the stadium was so shocked by his incredible performance.

He might have missed out on the world record by a couple of seconds, but Moses Kiptanui was now on the world stage to stay. One month later he won his first of three World Championships in Tokyo. The King of Steeplechase had arrived!

If he can do it, why can't I?

Twenty years after Moses Kiptanui's victory in Stockholm, I am standing outside the door of his office in the town of Eldoret, 30 minutes drive from Iten. His career long over, today he is a successful businessman running several companies.

He emerges to meet me – a tall, slim guy in a blue shirt with a red tie; immaculately well dressed.

'Welcome,' he says, flashing me the same broad smile that was transmitted around the globe as he stood atop the rostrum. 'Impressive' doesn't really do justice to this man's

CV. Three times world champion in the steeplechase. The first person on the planet to break the eight-minute barrier in the steeplechase, and the thirteen-minute barrier in the 5,000 metres. Years on, he is still in good shape, he tells me as we sit in the leather chairs in his office. Unlike the vast majority of Kenyan athletes, he has kept on training since he abandoned his career. He can still run 10 km in under 30 minutes, if he wants to. On the wall hangs a picture from one of his three steeplechase World Championships.

I ask him if that first win in Stockholm surprised him.

'Not at all. I had a strong conviction that I could win that race. Not winning was not an option,' he says, determination still etched across his face.

In those days there were no sports newspapers or television programmes covering athletics in Kenya. Nobody was seriously interested in the sport. But Moses Kiptanui and the others in the military camp in Nyahururu had heard about one or two men from the region who had made good money running in Europe. Apart from this, Moses knew that his younger cousin, Richard Chelimo (who would later hold the 10,000 metres world record), had won several races in Europe. As Moses puts it: 'I thought: what's so special about my cousin Richard? He's shorter than me and he wins. If he can do it, why can't I?'

Everyone wants to set a world record

Moses Kiptanui illustrates the invincible self-belief with which the Kenyan runners attack their careers. As an American athletics coach told me a couple of weeks before I travelled to Kenya: 'Virtually every running rookie in Kenya wants to set a world record or win a major city marathon,

119

and believes this is a viable proposition. On the other hand, having spent years lecturing runners in New York for the New York Road Runners, I have found that by far the most common goal there is merely to complete a race.'

It is this almost naive belief people have in their own abilities that I meet time and time again in Kenya. I get the first hint of this on the bus on my way back from Moses Kiptanui's office. The woman sitting next to me turns out to be Salina Kosgei, winner of numerous major marathons across the world. Then, having given birth to two children, she made a comeback and won the Boston Marathon in 2009. This is by no means rare in Iten. Female Kenyan runners are convinced that they can rejoin the world elite after they have given birth to their first child, and they actually do.

But where does this cast-iron certainty come from? What makes Salina and the other Kenyan women so convinced that they can win again after being out of training, often for several years? And why didn't Moses Kiptanui doubt for a second that he could win at Stockholm when he did not know his competitors and had never previously run in Europe?

Kenyans don't tolerate losing to a foreigner

The first person I meet on my return to the training camp is one of the foreign runners there. He is a rangy white guy with long grey hair gathered in a ponytail. The other runners here call him Jesus, but his real name is Toby Tanser. A globetrotter and long-distance runner with Swedish roots, he usually lives in New York. He came to Kenya for the first time in 1995 to pitch himself against the world's best runners. He became so infatuated with Kenyan running wisdom that he has written two books about it and comes every year to train in Iten. He laughs in agreement when I start talking about the Kenyans' extreme self-confidence.

'People come here looking for special genes,' he says. 'But what they find is people who simply do not believe they can lose. The Kenyans simply regard themselves as the world's undisputed rulers of middle- and long-distance running.'

This unshakeable belief in their own abilities has been built up layer upon layer in Kenya, as they have watched one countryman after another winning a gold medal over the last twenty years. As Toby puts it: 'You have to understand that many of them have never seen a white runner beat a Kenyan, and they won't tolerate losing to a *msungu* [The Kenyan term for a person of foreign descent].'

When Tanser participated in the Kenyans' local competitions in the 90s, onlookers threw stones at the Kenyan runners running behind him.

'Although I'm a good runner who has won races in Scandinavia, in the mind of the Kenyan, a foreigner is not someone you lose to in running. They shouted "Shame on you, you are being beaten by a *msungu*, you are shaming Kenya!" at the runners trying to catch up with me.'

The power of the mind

The recipe for any top performance always contains a large dash of self-belief. In any field, from business and politics to sports and music, this ability to instil belief, both in yourself and in others, is crucial to success. Doubt, by contrast, can poison any performance. One of the main reasons for people failing to achieve what they otherwise could is that they doubt their own abilities. When we doubt we get tense, fear the worst and multiply the probability of failure.

The most famous evidence of the power of belief is to be found in medicine. You've probably heard of the phenomenon of the placebo effect. In his renowned report, 'Psychological Variables in Human Cancer' in 1957, the psychologist Bruno Klopfer describes a man to whom his doctors referred as 'Mr Wright'. Mr Wright had far-advanced lymph sarcoma with tumours the size of oranges in his neck, groin, chest and armpits. He had already exhausted all known treatments and was expected to die in the not-too-distant future.

Nevertheless, Mr Wright was confident that a new anti-cancer drug called Krebiozen would cure him. He was already bedridden and fighting for every breath when he received his first injection of what he believed was Krebiozen – in fact it was water. Dr Klopfer expected him to be dead within a few days but instead was amazed to find him out of his bed happily chatting away, joking with the nurses. Mr Wright's tumours had shrunk by half, and after ten more days of treatment he was discharged from the hospital. However, the other patients in the hospital who had received Krebiozen showed no improvement at all.

Within a few months negative reports began to appear in the media about the effectiveness of the drug. Mr Wright relapsed to his original state and returned to hospital, depressed and close to death once more. At this point Dr Klopfer assured Mr Wright that the bad press was due to early shipments of the drug deteriorating during transit, and promised to treat him with some fresh, extra-potent

Krebiozen. Mr Wright regained his positive attitude and again he responded to the treatment with amazing results. He did not know that the injections he received were actually only water.

Mr Wright's story is by no means exceptional. The power of belief making ill people well again has been documented again and again. It used to be generally thought that placebo effects were just a case of people's perception of their own illness changing. However, research has shown several biological effects that placebos can exert. Brain chemicals, stress hormones and the immune system can all be influenced by the power of belief. People with Parkinson's disease given placebo injections showed significantly higher dopamine levels in the brain. It's a fiction that results in measurable, factual results – that's the paradox of the placebo effect. It has basically nothing to do with the pharmacological properties of whatever 'drug' is used. The effect primarily derives from the 'false' belief that the 'drug' is effective.

Performance placebo

I lie on my modest wooden bed in my little room at the training camp, thinking. My meetings with Moses Kiptanui, Salina Kosgei and Toby Tanser have made me wonder whether the Kenyans have simply created their own collective performance placebo effect. Perhaps it is this more than anything else that separates them from other runners. Maybe their irrational belief in their own abilities enables them to achieve the apparently impossible. Take the former 5,000 metres world champion, Benjamin Limo, for example. He had no TV, only a radio, but through it he had heard how all the Kenyans won gold medals at the 1988 Olympics. Every time he turned on the radio, another Kenyan had won. So he thought that all he actually needed to do was to get to the Olympics – once he was there he would win for sure.

Such is life in Iten. Living there, you are constantly bombarded with the message that you too can achieve something big. To Kenyans, the possibility of losing simply does not exist. As Toby Tanser told me:

'A few years back I said to some of my Kenyan friends that I would show them a white person who could beat every Kenyan. They were all about to fall off their chairs laughing. "A white man cannot defeat the Kenyans!" they shouted. I asked if they were prepared to bet 50 shillings each. Although none of them had a penny to their name, they all took the bet, they were that convinced. "Nobody can beat Paul Bitok of the Nandi tribe," they said. But I had a video tape from the 1992 Olympics in Barcelona, in which Dieter Bauman sprints past the Kenyans to win the 5,000 metres. When I inserted the tape and they saw that I was right they were left in complete shock. This is a good example of the brainwashing that goes on here, which is a highly underestimated factor in Kenyan success.'

It is also interesting to note that the Kenyans' belief in their own abilities is not really founded on logical, rational analysis of the way things are. If anything, the opposite is true. Just think of Moses Kiptanui. He did not even consider the possibility of defeat in Stockholm, yet in reality there was a strong chance that he could lose. Or Benjamin Limo. In actual fact, is it is simply not true that all the Kenyans returned home from the Olympics with a medal. Many of them got nowhere close. But because the radio was his only source of information, he developed an over-whelmingly positive impression of the performance of the Kenyan athletes.

Neither Moses Kiptanui nor Benjamin Limo based their beliefs on logical assessment of the facts. But even if they weren't necessarily correct, their 'truths' gave them the faith and the courage to do the impossible. As Matthew Syed puts it in his book *Bounce*: 'The paradoxical conclusion behind the performance placebo effect is that the thing that often separates the best from the rest is a capacity to believe things that are not true, but which are incredibly effective.' In other words: it is not a question of being right, it is a question of winning.

The downside of knowledge

The Kenyan runners challenge the rational, analytical Western approach to developing top performance. Those who know the most (or think they do) are not necessarily those who win. In the West we have masses of knowledge and scientific ballast, yet in Kenya they have the results. Perhaps too much knowledge and information can actually limit potential, instead of helping to unlock it.

Colm O'Connell, the Godfather of Kenyan running, had this to say on the subject: 'Americans and Europeans analyse everything. They break an athlete down into atoms. Here is your maximum oxygen uptake, here is your muscle fibre type distribution, over here you can see your pulse, and by the way, one of your legs is longer than the other. I think that kind of over-analysis destroys an athlete. I accept them as they are. If I start making my athletes too aware, I remove their instinctive drive and self-belief.'

All this is not to say that knowledge, information and a degree of realism are not useful qualities. Every top performer has to make rational choices, evaluate themselves critically and be able to stare reality in the face, but too much information can damage their chances by narrowing their perceptions of what is achievable.

In the words of Colm O'Connell: 'Athletes don't respond well to too much information. You must only give them a minimum. If one of my athletes has a problem I don't necessarily tell them so. Instead I get them to train in a way I think will solve it, without making them aware of it. The last thing I want them to think ahead of an important competition is that they have a problem. There is a feel-good factor which you have to be aware of.'

The question is whether this simplicity and minimum of information is one of the Kenyan runners' best-kept secrets? For example, nobody in Kenya tells you that you need slim calves or unusually high oxygen uptake to join the world elite. Nobody's maximum oxygen uptake is even measured. Here everyone is like Moses Kiptanui; they look at the success stories and think, 'If they can do it, why can't I?'

See it before it happens

If you want to foster self-belief it is crucial to realise that the human mind doesn't respond as well to information and facts as it does to stories and images. As Colm O'Connell expresses it: 'Don't start with knowledge! Start with desire and imagination, then knowledge will come.'

Albert Einstein seems to have been in agreement, once saying: 'Imagination is more important than knowledge.'

You have to first be able to imagine something before you will be able to turn that thing into reality. One of the best-known studies of the power of imagination – or visualisation as sport psychologists name it – was conducted by Dr Judd Blaslotto at the University of Chicago. He split a basketball team into three groups and tested each one to see how many points they could score with a limited number of free throws. After this, he had the first group practise free throws every day for an hour. The second group just *visualised* themselves making free throws. The third group did nothing. After 30 days, he tested them again. As expected the third group did not improve at all. The first group had improved by 24 per cent, and incredibly the second group had improved by 23 per cent *without touching a basketball*!

Bizarre as it may sound, in some disciplines it seems to be possible to achieve a similar effect from visualisation as from certain types of training. In another study, Alvaro Pascual-Leone, a Harvard neuroscientist, divided volunteers into two groups. The first group was given a five-finger piano exercise to practise for two hours for five days a week. At the end of each session Pascual-Leone measured the neural activation of the group. He noticed that even after just five days of practice new neural circuits were being established.

The second group was asked to simply imagine playing the same piano piece each day. When he measured this group's neural activation he found that mere mental rehearsal of playing the piano had altered the same physical structures and established neural circuits in the same way that actual practice had with the first group. Even more thought-provoking was the fact that the performances of the two groups were almost identical when they were tested after a two-week period.

These studies demonstrate the power of visualisation and mental practice, and they show us in concrete terms that the limits of possibility can be, and indeed are, altered by your mind.

Walt Disney clearly understood the importance of visualisation – he once said that if he had not seen Disneyland in his mind, the rest of the world would not have seen it on Earth. The clarity of the mental picture he had helped him to bounce back from all the setbacks he met along the way.

Swimmer Michael Phelps, eight times gold winner at the Beijing Olympics, has described the part played by visualisation in his success, too: 'There are times in my sleep when I literally dream my race from start to finish. Other nights ... I visualise to the point that I know exactly what I want to do: dive, glide, stroke, flip, reach the wall, hit the split time to the hundredth, then swim back again for as many times as I need to finish.'

In sports this is often referred to as the Bannister Effect after the British doctor Roger Bannister. In 1965 he became the first man to break the four-minute mile, with a time of 3 minutes 59.4 seconds. Until then, it was widely believed that it was physically impossible for a man to run a mile in less than four minutes. People claimed the human body would burst from such a trial of speed and endurance.

The most incredible part of this story is not Bannister's achievement, but the effect it had on other runners. Forty-six days after the record-breaking event, the Australian John Landy bettered Bannister's time, managing 3 minutes 57.9 seconds. Within two years, 37 runners had broken the four-minute mile. The reason was certainly not physical conditioning, better tracks or improved shoes. The real barrier to break wasn't physical, but mental. Bannister's success removed a mental block from thousands of other runners, allowing them to believe that they could match and even better his achievement.

Meet four world record holders in 30 minutes

This is exactly what goes on every single day in the Kenyan running Gold Mine in Iten. You constantly hear people's stories of neighbours, cousins, uncles and friends who made it. I still remember my first early morning training session there. Although I felt in good shape, I was overtaken by one group of runners after another. My surprise was not so much due to being overtaken as to the personalities who ran past me. First came Olympic gold medallist Asbel Kiprop, and after him three world record holders – first Linet Masai, then Mary Keitany and Florence Kiplagat.

It wasn't until later in my stay that I realised that was just a perfectly ordinary morning in Iten. If you go jogging for 30 minutes as the sun rises, meeting four world champions on the way is not an exceptional event. In Iten the superstars train side-by-side with the young hopefuls. Imagine what that means. Every morning, the novices get to see how the world's best do their training. They see that elite runners also suffer when the going gets tough; that they are not always at their best either – they see that they are humans too. But they also see what price they are willing to pay and how hard they push themselves. They witness what it takes to success at close quarters.

This is precisely what gave Moses Kiptanui the conviction that he could win in Stockholm. It's also the mechanism that instilled self-belief in Wilson Kipketer, the treble world champion and former world record holder for the 800 metres. As he told me: 'I was a student at St Patrick's High School in Iten, and realising that Peter Rono [Olympic gold medallist in the 1,500 metres] went to the same school made a big difference to me. He slept in the same building as me, we ate the same food and we had same coach. That made me think: if he could do it, I can do it too.'

It's easy to see how this applies in contexts outside of athletics. Since Apple released the iPad the market has been inundated with similar tablets from other companies. Those companies all had what they needed to release the first tablet, but didn't until Apple showed them the way with the iPad.

When you're pursuing a goal, there is something reassuring in knowing there is someone who has done it before, whatever it might be. Knowing that it's possible and studying how it was done will almost certainly increase the chances of you remaining committed.

Shoals of stars

There are a lot of things we believe to be impossible only because we haven't seen anyone do them. When we're struggling with a project or a problem, the likeliest reason for giving up is the belief that it can't be done. What's the point of persevering and investing time if it's actually impossible to succeed? If you are presented with convincing evidence that it *can* be done, it's not an impossible task any longer. For most people, just knowing that something really is possible makes the idea of doing it themselves seem achievable. It removes the mental block that prevents them from succeeding. Understand this mechanism and you've understood a key ingredient of any Gold Mine.

When Russian tennis star Anna Kournikova reached the semi-finals at Wimbledon in 1997, there were no other Russian players in the world top ten. Two years after Kournikova's breakthrough, there were five.

Similarly, when the South Korean golfer Se Ri Pak became Rookie of the Year on the LPGA Tour in 1998 she was the only South Korean golfer in the world top 100. Today, just over ten years later, 35 per cent of the world's 100 best golfers are South Koreans.

In the late 1980s Korea had fewer than 200 golfers between the ages of fifteen and eighteen able to do a round under par. Today, the country has more than 3,000 young golfers with a handicap of zero or less, and the National Korean PGA Tour pumps out superstars. It is unlikely that Se Ri Pak expected to ignite such a fire when she won her Rookie of the Year prize, but the nation's driving ranges were quickly flooded with young girls who wanted to be the best in the world and were convinced they could make it. The first lady of South Korean golf had paved the way for her sisters, and the rest is history. Since 1998, seven out of the eleven rookie prizes have been won by a South Korean woman.

It is perhaps difficult for us to understand this kind of sudden blossoming of talent. After all, in a sense nothing had changed in these places. In Russia the rackets were the same, the courts looked no different and the training regimen was the same. In South Korea the clubs and courses remained the same, as did the players' genes. The transformation was in the attitudes of the athletes. Having seen what could be achieved, they set out to emulate that success themselves. The raw ability to play tennis and golf was already there, but their self-belief exploded.

As the elite South Korean player Mi-Hyun Kim told me: 'Before Se Ri made it on to the LPGA Tour, we all thought that was something huge; something we couldn't achieve. But after she won two majors in her first year, some of us started to think that maybe we could do the same.'

Each of the Gold Mines seems to have its own Se Ri Pak. In Ethiopia it was Abebe Bikila, the first black African to win an Olympic gold medal. In Brazil it was the football legend Pelé. And in Kenya it was Kipchoge Keino, who won gold in the 1,500 metres at the 1968 Mexico City Olympics. Once a single person has pushed the limits of what is possible, ten more will follow in their slipstream.

This, more than anything else, is the secret behind the winning culture in the Gold Mines. Each successive star paves the road on which the stars of the future will tread. They make others see and believe that the impossible is possible, fostering their ability to visualise success. When you are only a few strides away from a training partner who has run a 2.04 marathon, or set a new world record, there is every reason to believe you are equally capable.

There was a similar phenomenon in the 1990s where Santa Monica Track club achieved total domination in the sprints, with Carl Lewis at the fore. In those days there would be a world champion or an Olympic medallist in practically every one of the eight lanes. It was a fact that if you 'won' the Tuesday night starting practice then you were the world's fastest athlete off the blocks. When you find yourself in that kind of environment your preconceptions about your own abilities and limits are completely rewritten. You can give a person the most sophisticated education and conditioning but nothing beats planting them in an environment with people who do what they want to do, but who are better at it than they are.

Sessions of suffering

On my second day in Iten I get another demonstration of the Kenyans' irrational, instinctive relationship to what is possible and how it puts them in a different league to everybody else. My alarm goes off at 5.30 a.m. I have agreed to meet a group of Kenyan runners outside the camp. I wipe the sleep out of my eyes and groggily get out of bed, trying to motivate my tired body by focusing on what Moses Kiptanui told me on my first day in Kenya: 'There will be training sessions out on the red paths that you will never forget. You'll find the going tough, but the scenery is incredible and you will be in the company of record holders and Olympic gold winners.'

Twenty minutes later I'm standing outside the metal gate at the entrance to the camp waiting for my training group to arrive. All around I see runners trickling over the undulating landscape like tiny ants. Iten is a running farm, created by the athletes themselves. Young hopefuls flock here to become part of the training environment. Even though everybody competes against everybody else, there is a special sense of cohesion here. Even the poorest runners will find somewhere to sleep here and some ugali to eat.

The East African runners push their limits mentally as well as physically

My training group suddenly appears in the early morning light. 'Come on!' shouts the runner at the front of the pack, and I join in at the back.

All the runners in this area follow more or less the same regimen. Most of them train three times a day: an early session at 6 a.m., the next at 10 a.m. and the last late in the afternoon. Every Tuesday, several hundred runners of all ages gather at the only track in Iten, which is more a 400-metre potholed dirt road than a proper athletics track. This is where the Kenyans run their famous, much feared interval races. It is not unusual to see people run until they retch, only to get up and run on. As Toby Tanser puts it: 'Here I see runners suffer to a degree that I cannot in my wildest dreams imagine anybody in the West subjecting themselves to. This is a fast moving journey which wrenches the body beyond its mortal limitations; it starts with the recognition that pain is the validation of accomplishment.'

Knowing too much

We have now been running for 45 minutes through the countryside and the sun is beating down on us from a cloud-free sky. The group has drastically increased its pace. The most recent gear change has taken me right into the red zone. My heart is galloping and I am gasping for breath in the thin air. Even though the group has been very considerate of the new white boy in the class, I am forced to throw the towel in five minutes later. I jog back towards the camp completely shattered, while the group briskly disappears out of view. When Kenya's former marathon record holder Paul Tergat was asked about the secret of the Kenyans' success he replied simply: 'If you train with us you will see why we win.' He was right.

Another thing I notice is that nobody runs with a heart rate monitor in Iten. In fact, the only heart rate monitor I see during my stay has been taken apart by its owner so he can use it as a line to dry his wet clothes. Colm O'Connell smiles broadly when I confess that I am amazed at the absence of a piece of equipment that would be considered standard in the West. 'Fifteen years ago I was given a heart rate monitor by some Swedish scientists,' he says. 'I've still got it; it's still in the box in my room. Here, nobody needs a heart rate monitor to tell them that there is no more petrol in the tank.'

The use of computers is now becoming commonplace in the Western world. Runners return from their workouts to feed all kinds of data into a training log, often downloading it from their watches. The Kenyans, however, keep their training much simpler. There nobody allows a heart rate monitor to tell them how hard they can train or what their physical limitations are. As Toby Tanser explains: 'Scientists will always maintain that if the Kenyans ran according to the scientifically "correct" method, they would run even faster. If Martin Lel had been born in the United States, they would have thrown him straight into the weight training room, but the fact is that he has never been to a gym and yet he has won the London Marathon three times and the New York City Marathon twice. Kenyans are not scientific. They are instinctive, organic runners who know a hell of a lot about running and the body's potential with no knowledge of expressions like VO_2 max, lactic acid or anatomy.'

The moment of truth

Paradoxically enough, some of the most powerful evidence as to why the Kenyans' somewhat irrational attitude allows them to win is to be found in rational science. South African professor of exercise and sports science Tim Noakes has done some fascinating work in this area.

In his late twenties Noakes started to become interested in running. Today he has run more than 70 marathon and ultra-marathon races, is author of the book *Lore of Running* and has been recognised the world over for his Central Governor Model, which maintains that the brain – and not the body, as was previously believed – is the primary organ that dictates how fast, how long and how hard humans can exercise.

If you run 1,000 metres as fast as you can you will begin at some point to feel discomfort and fatigue. However, according to Noakes that feeling of tiredness does not come from the muscles, but from the brain. Basically, the brain tries to protect itself and avoid you pushing yourself so hard that you reach the finish line in an exhausted or damaged state. It therefore makes you feel tired, and it is because of this control mechanism that we don't generally run to the point of complete breakdown. In other words: when you're so tired that it feels like you're about to collapse any second, you're actually not even remotely close to your limit. Tim Noakes says: 'I don't see fatigue as a physical phenomenon; I see it purely as an emotion. You have to understand that however bad you feel, it's actually just your brain playing a trick on you to make sure you don't damage yourself. You always have a little in reserve, or as some would interpret this, you can always push yourself a bit harder.'

According to Noakes, succumbing to fatigue is nothing more or less than quitting. What we call exhaustion is not the inability to continue; it's basically giving up. 'I can show you a lot of videos where the distance at the finish line between the first and the second runner is inches. In these cases the second runner chooses to lose, he chooses to come second. It's not that the athlete didn't have reserves. He just didn't manage to activate those reserves. His brain said no because he wasn't able to convince himself that it was important to go even deeper. He accepted coming second.'

The rise of a scientific revolution

Tim Noakes's idea that it is your mind that limits your performance rather than the actual capability of your muscles is supported by more recent findings. In a study published in 2011 in the European Journal of Applied Physiology, Samuele Marcora, an exercise physiologist at Bangor University in Wales, brought ten elite rugby players into her lab and had them perform a simple exercise protocol in three steps. First they pedalled on a stationary bike as hard as they could for five seconds while their power output was recorded (a test of maximal voluntary cycling power, or MVCP).

After a period of rest they were then required to pedal the same bikes for as long as possible at a fixed intensity that corresponded to 90 per cent of their individual VO_2 maximum values. Marcora offered cash prizes to the top performers and circulated the results publicly to stimulate competition and make sure the subjects went all-out and rode to exhaustion. The players were also asked to rate their exhaustion on a scale of 6 to 20 (20 being complete exhaustion). On average, they rated themselves at 19.6 on that scale.

Immediately after completing this ride to exhaustion, each of the players then repeated the five-second maximum power test. Not surprisingly, Marcora found that, on average, the rugby players cycled with 30 per cent less power in the final five-second MVCP-test (performed in a state of exhaustion) than they did in the first MVCP (performed in a fresh state). On the other hand, it also transpired that they pedalled with three times as much power in the final five-second MVCP-test (performed in a state of exhaustion) than they managed in their fixed-intensity ride to complete exhaustion. But how were the rugby players able to triple their power output when they were already in a state of near total exhaustion? If they had stopped their ride to exhaustion because they were no longer physically able to sustain their performance, how could they then drastically improve on that performance immediately afterwards, without any opportunity to rest?

You're a quitter

Marcora's findings stand in sharp contrast to the traditional way of explaining tiredness. Explanations are usually based on the conviction that a decrease in performance is the result of physical fatigue – pointing to the fact that less oxygen reaches the muscles, that lactic acid builds up and that our legs tire.

It is upon this traditional view that all product development in the running industry is based. It has led to the development of countless methods to augment training, such as heart rate monitors, eating carbohydrates to replenish glycogen in tired muscles and even blood doping to allow more oxygen to be carried to active muscles. But if it were a physical barrier which limited performance it would not be possible for the rugby players to triple their power after having rated themselves as being almost completely exhausted, with nothing left to give. If their muscles were truly able to do no more, that last push would be impossible.

Marcora's studies have paved the way for a revolution in the way we view fatigue, convincingly arguing that its true cause is the perception of effort. People give up way before they have reached their absolute physiological limit. The rugby players certainly didn't feel as if they quit voluntarily. When they struggled in the exhaustion ride and couldn't sustain the intensity any longer despite their best efforts, it *felt* as though it was their bodies that had reached a limit, but in reality it was their minds giving up – something of a paradox. The next time you feel as though you have reached your absolute limit in some activity, stop and ask yourself – have you really?

Intensity is king

The idea that the brain to a large extent sets limits for the body makes self-confidence and mental toughness seem even more crucial for the development of world-class performance than it was previously thought. It also explains why exercise physiologists have had trouble explaining the fact that high-level endurance athletes aren't very different from each other when they undergo different physiological tests – there are no discernable differences between the winners and the losers. They all have a very high VO_2 max, demonstrate good running economy and so on. It is impossible to explain the difference between their performances purely on the basis of physiological parameters. The difference between the best and the next best is more likely to be psychological.

Samuele Marcora also carried out a number of tests to gauge athletes' perceptions of their own abilities, or what psychologists refer to as self-efficacy. The tests showed that beliefs about personal limits tend to be self-fulfilling. People who think they are able to push harder and do more, usually can.

This, of course, takes us right back to the Kenyans and their apparently irrational approach to training. Tim Noakes explains it like this: 'If you look at Kenyan runners, they have a different attitude to pain and they push behind intensity of training to a whole new level. When they start feeling discomfort, I don't think that they see it as pain in the same way than others do. They see it as a challenge. '

The marathon triple world champion Paul Tergat says more or less the same thing: 'Hard training is all about asking yourself: can I give more? The answer is usually yes.'

How to delay being tired

Every time I asked European athletes who train or have trained in Iten about their experience of the Kenyan method, I was met with resigned looks and shakes of the head: 'They just push, push, push and then keep pushing,' they said.

You can see fear in the eyes of Western athletes who go

to Iten to train when the subject of the Kenyans' merciless interval running training comes up. When European and American athletes come to train, they often ask the coach: 'How many intervals are we going to have today?' No Kenyans ever ask that question. Nobody knows how many intervals they will have to run and nobody asks how many are left. They run right to the edge of collapse, perhaps lying in a ditch retching afterwards, only to get up to run once more.

Another good example of the Kenyan refusal to discount anything as impossible is the game 'Catch the Impala', one of their 'alternative' training methods, particularly popular among the Nandi people.

The impala is a type of antelope and a supremely fast animal, but it doesn't have much staying power. If you run after it, it will stop at some stage to rest. Then, before you get too close it will start running again. Assuming the impala manages to have these rests, this stop-and-start chase can go on for about 40 km. After that point the impala is very tired and if you have the speed and endurance you may be able to get close enough to pat it on the backside. To the Kenyans, 'Catch the Impala' is the ultimate test of manhood – as the former Olympic 800 metres bronze winner Mark Coty once said: 'When I returned home to Kenya, they actually respected me more for my ability to catch an impala than for having brought home an Olympic medal.'

The idea that a person running on foot would be able to catch a wild animal as fast as the impala seems incredible; so incredible that most of us would dismiss it as impossible. By not accepting what we would consider to be obvious human limitations, the Kenya runners make the impossible possible.

A world without limits

The power of positive thinking which allows the Kenyans to push beyond apparent boundaries has implications far beyond the sporting world. The main reason that people – or organisations for that matter – do not achieve the success they desire is usually the story they tell themselves about why it cannot be done. They don't have the right training or education, the state of the market is not on their side, they don't have enough money or resources, they don't live in the right place, the last time they tried they didn't succeed – an endless list of reasons to fail. All these explanations serve no purpose other than to excuse people for not trying, or rather not committing themselves completely. Explanations like these make us quitters!

In reality, this starts early on. From the day we are born we pick up ideas, attitudes and convictions from the world around us. Our parents, friends, teachers, the media and many other sources all try to sell us their version of the truth. The truth we consciously or unconsciously choose to accept forms our convictions as to what is possible and what is not. The problem is that many people end up accepting a 'truth' that limits them rather than opening up possibilities for them.

This is difficult to avoid. From the moment we get up to the time we go to bed, we are bombarded with information that makes us feel limited. The media, for example, serve up one depressing piece of news after another about the global financial crisis and the hovering threat of recession. If we are programmed to feel that we are in an environment in which it is impossible to succeed then of course we are likely to resign ourselves to failure. Just take a look at Greece, struggling for survival and on the brink of state bankruptcy. Without doubt, the country is in a state of deep financial crisis, but it is in just as deep a psychological crisis. The Greeks are subjected to a deluge of bad news every day, even though there are also positive cases of Greeks defying the crisis and building successful companies. This atmosphere strangles any form of initiative, it pacifies people – bad news rapidly develops into self-fulfilling prophecy.

Anyone who wants to develop high performance should be aware of this danger. We are all at risk of becoming psychological quitters. Subconscious programming and an overload of limiting information can paralyse people's imagination and drive. The result is that we end up performing in a box created for us by others, a box that is far too small.

It happens in all spheres of life, and particularly in the education system. As the world-renowned creativity expert Ken Robinson once said: 'We are educating people out of their creativity.'

We are being trained to dream small dreams, but small dreams represent an attitude of fear. They sabotage our imagination and keep us from setting new standards and acquiring new skills. Just think of all the art we haven't seen yet, the jobs that haven't been created yet and the records that haven't been broken yet.

My point is that if a culture becomes too regulated, information-heavy and realistic there is a risk that it will lose the irrational optimism needed to break records. As we gain more experience and knowledge we lose our naivety, and that is not necessarily a good thing. This kind of naivety characterises the entrepreneurs, leaders, architects, artists and athletes who genuinely push the limits of what is possible. The challenge therefore is to maintain our naivety while continuing to harvest more experience and knowledge. Colm O'Connell puts it beautifully: 'When you are young, you are running with your heart. When you grow older, you start running with your brain. You start calculating and worrying if the pace is too fast, or if you might sustain an injury. As a youngster you just go out and do it. My job is to keep the youthful aggressive instinct alive in my athletes when they grow older.'

Any organisation or culture that wants to attain new heights and set new standards must foster and stimulate naivety and the ability to think without limitations. To achieve the extraordinary, people need the ability to believe *despite* the facts and not *because of* them. Dean Keith Simonton, a professor of psychology at University of California at Davis, has identified this as an extremely common characteristic among high achievers. As he puts it: 'They really believe that in the end that they're going to win, and until they do, they will keep on pushing, keep on making the phone calls, writing the letters, whatever it takes.'

You will always be able to find 100 reasons that something isn't possible, but there will also always be at least one good reason that it is. For this reason I am convinced that we can learn far more from running in Kenya than from laboratories in the West. Iten is a world where you will never hear why something is not possible. There is room for big dreams.

Just remember that dreamers don't have special genes. They are simply determined and relentless in chasing those those dreams. If my cousin Richard can do it, why can't I?

What you should never forget about BELIEF

1. Imagination is more important than knowledge. If you can't visualise it happening, it will not happen. Anyone wanting to break records and push boundaries must build a clear picture in their mind of what they want to achieve.

2. Too much information and knowledge can limit potential, paralyse action and kill belief. A top performer must distinguish between what they really need to know and what is just nice to know.

3. Belief is not about being right. It's about winning. What often separates the best from the rest is a capacity to believe things that are logically not true, but which are powerfully motivating.

4. Be realistic, but be unrealistic at the same time. Any organisation wishing to deliver high performance must nurture its ability to think on an unrealistically large scale and stimulate its naivety about what's possible.

Success is about mindset, not facilities

'Talent tends to get in the way of itself. I often think that people succeed more despite their talent than because of it.'

Won Park, golf coach in the South Korean Gold Mine

My taxi swings through the gates of the University of Technology in Kingston. The light from its left headlight – the only one that works – lights up the road in front of us as we trundle through the desolate university park.

The rumble of the engine and the reggae music emanating from the car's speakers are the only sounds here – it's really early, and the first students will not check in to the university for several hours. We come to a standstill in front of a rusty fence that surrounds what looks like a grass field.

'We're here,' says my driver, sticking out his left hand towards me for payment.

Am I really in the right place, I wonder? I hesitate for moment before paying the driver and getting out of the car. I've come to visit the world's most successful athletics club, the MVP Track and Field Club, and I have been told that they train here at the university grounds. But there is no athletics track here. No streetlights either. As I get closer I catch a glimpse of some runners moving in the darkness beyond the fence. Once my eyes have grown accustomed to the gloom I can see about 40 athletes out on the grass.

The famous grass track at MVP

If you started to talk about the world's most progressive athletics club, most people would imagine a first-class college with cutting-edge facilities. But there is no high-tech test equipment here, no cutting-edge fitness centre – not even an athletics track. Just a pile of cones, a stopwatch, some rusty old weights in a dilapidated fitness shed with no air conditioning and a poor quality 400-metre grass track. Nevertheless, it is here that world record holders, Olympic gold medallists and world champions train.

And Stephen Francis, the founder of the club, has no intention of changing anything: 'A performance environment should not be designed for comfort but for hard work,' he tells me. 'It has to show people that the road to success is long and uncomfortable.'

Stephen Francis and his team at the first training session of the day

A performer must not feel too comfortable

The ethos with which Stephen Francis runs the MVP Track and Field Club seriously challenges the modern Western mindset. We seem to believe groomed fields, top-level technology and comfortable surroundings are necessary prerequisites for success. We would tend to use poor, overcrowded facilities as an excuse for not achieving better results.

Just think of the famous Chelsea FC Football Academy

which has spent nigh on £100 million building a state-of-the-art training centre in London's prosperous commuter belt. The club has scoured Europe for talented kids between the ages of twelve and eighteen and bought them for millions of pounds. At the academy they arrive for training in taxis and are served food prepared by a three-star chef between sessions. When touring abroad they stay in luxury hotels. The results of Chelsea's talent strategy have so far been about as bleak as a winter day in the Russian wilderness where owner Roman Abramovich grew up. Not a single player from the academy has managed to make his mark in Chelsea's Premier League team. John Terry, who signed a professional contract in 1997 (six years before Abramovich arrived in London), is the last player to come through the academy and become a first-team regular. In other words, Roman Abramovich could just as well be throwing his £100 million at the roulette wheel of a casino in Moscow.

This over-emphasis on comfort and super modern facilities is, however, not just a talent strategy predominant in the world of sport. In the business world, companies invest fortunes in spectacular office moves, despite the fact that all the research shows that doing so does not improve performance. They just carry the same problems with them. Other companies send their so-called greatest talents to luxurious spa hotels for away days while they tell them how fantastic they are, lulling them into complacency.

Is there any foundation for the assumption that we develop better performance in fancy facilities? Or might it actually be more productive to train in the kind of humble conditions which Stephen Francis insists on. Perhaps luxurious surroundings diminish effort, because they leave people with a feeling that nobody striving for top performance should ever have: that of already having arrived.

As Stephen Francis says: 'I don't think they've got that message in the United States, Australia, Sweden, England, et cetera. When they build big smart training centres they are trying to make life as comfortable as possible for the athletes. But that's not right. The athletes must demonstrate that they are so keen to succeed that they will ignore the fact that they could have found better, more comfortable conditions elsewhere.'

This makes the world's most successful sprint coach sound like a dictatorial drill sergeant, driving his recruits through meaningless physical tests in order to break them down psychologically. However, behind Stephen Francis's provocative words lie intelligent considerations as to how one can make people reveal what it is that drives them simply through their actions. Francis uses the Spartan conditions to identify factors you cannot read from a certificate, construe from a psychological profile analysis or ask your way to in a job interview. He uses his facilities to penetrate the glossy surface to find out the answer to the critical questions: why are you here, really? How much do you care? What are you prepared to give – and to sacrifice? In other words: who really wants it most?

As he says: 'By keeping my facilities humble I maintain the focus on what it's all about, and I automatically separate off athletes who may be good sprinters but who are more driven by smart facilities, fame and comfort than the will to improve themselves.'

The conviction Stephen Francis wants to implant in the subconscience of his sprinters is crystal clear: success is not about facilities, it's about mindset.

The rusty gym at MVP

The MVP training ground

The wonder child

It is an uncomfortably cold November evening, just a week after my return from Jamaica. I am standing at the edge of an Astroturf pitch in Northern Denmark. I've come here to see what most people would categorise as a completely routine reserve team match in the Danish league. Only fifteen spectators have decided to brave the cold, probably because the players are of a relatively low standard – the teams are a mixture of ditched players in serious need of match training, a handful of under-eighteen lads wanting to show off a bit and a couple of players who need to be tested in a match with not too much at stake. One of these is the 22-year-old American Freddy Adu who is being tried out by Randers FC, offering him the chance of an anonymous existence at the bottom of the Danish league. Freddy's the one I'm here to see. Ten metres away from me, he is jogging to warm up. I wonder what's on his mind. Is he trying to motivate himself to play in this totally uninspiring setting? Perhaps worrying about why there's no crowd? Or maybe he's thinking back to the time when major clubs all over the globe were on their knees trying to get to him to sign with them.

Nine years previously when he was just twelve years old he was the main guest on David Letterman's *Late Show*. It must have been overwhelming, but Freddy seemed to enjoy it all, sitting there with a charming grin while the audience clapped and the host presented him as the 'New Pelé'.

The new Pelé is born

Freddy Adu was born in Ghana on 2 June 1989. He lived with his family in Tema, a busy harbour town on Ghana's

THE GOLD MINE EFFECT

Atlantic coast. It was here that he started to play football, spending hours at a time kicking a ball about barefoot in the streets. When he was eight, Freddy moved to the United States after his family won a green card lottery.

They settled in the Washington D.C. area, but life was not easy. Shortly after their arrival, Freddy's father abandoned the family. His mum, Emilie, had to take several jobs in order to support her sons. However, it was not long before people began to notice Freddy's football skills, and at the age of just ten years old he helped his team to win in an under-14s tournament in Italy. He was pronounced the tournament's best player. This confirmed that he was one to watch, and back home in Washington the telephone began to ring off the hook. Agents, clubs, coaches – all of them wanted a share in the new Pelé. Freddy was that good. So good, in fact, that you could not turn on the American sports channel ESPN without hearing about him.

His play was of such a high standard that one expert even prophesied that he would have a place on the American team at the World Cup in 2006, at which time he would be just seventeen. This was the same age as Pelé when he made his debut in the World Cup finals in 1958. Even the then American A-team coach Bruce Arena was completely bowled over with admiration, saying: 'Freddy is undoubtedly the most talented player we have ever seen at that age.'

Interest in Freddy even spread across the Atlantic, and major Italian club Inter Milan made an offer of 750,000 dollars for the lad, an offer which Freddy and his mother refused. Sir Alex Ferguson would later reveal that Manchester United had also tried to get their hands on him.

To complete the list of admirers, Nike and Pepsi threw

advertising contracts worth millions at the twelve-year-old prodigy. In his first commercial, Freddy faces off with Pelé himself. Towards the end of the advert the legend looks his apprentice straight in the eye and says: 'Listen here, God has given you the gift to play football.'

Record gobbler

In this light, nobody was surprised when, at the age of fourteen, Freddy Adu became the United States' youngest ever athlete to sign a professional contract worth $500,000 a year. He had made his debut on the American under-17 team the previous year, just three weeks after becoming an American citizen.

Freddy toppled one record after another. On 3 April 2004 he made his debut as the youngest player ever in Major League Soccer. Two weeks later, on 17 April 2004, he became the youngest goal-scorer in the history of MLS. The world seemed to be witnessing the birth of a new legend. And Freddy himself was caught up in the excitement. As he said: 'I see myself in a World Cup final playing for the United States against a top team that everyone believes will win. And we'll just come along and take them completely unawares. One day, when I'm holding the World Cup trophy, somebody will come along and take a picture. It'll be so cool!'

How could we have been so terribly mistaken?

In the context of such a glittering past it is thought provoking, to say the least, that Freddy Adu is now standing on a wilderness of a football pitch out in the middle of nowhere. Why is he not performing conjuring tricks on the world's most famous football pitches as everyone predicted? Adu was nowhere to be seen on the American national team at the recent 2010 World Cup in South Africa.

The fact is that Freddy Adu has failed. Big time. Sir Alex Ferguson, Pelé, Nike and the others are all dumbfounded. After two seasons with European clubs like SL Benfica and AS Monaco he had, by and large, not played in the starting line-up. After that he was on loan to a minor club in the Greek second division, followed by a stint at an even less significant club in the second best Turkish league. Even at this level he was found wanting. Randers FC in Denmark was far from impressed, and two months after I witnessed him play, Freddy was sent back to Philadelphia Union in the American Major League where everything began.

But what went wrong? How could Freddy Adu fall from being the wonder kid of the footballing world to a career nobody is likely to remember? It seems astonishing that his development should have come to such a disastrous halt, and that so many experts and coaches were so grossly mistaken about him.

We can find the answers to this conundrum at Stanford University.

She made them liars

Carol Dweck is a 63-year-old psychologist at Stanford who has spent more than 30 years carrying out systematic research into why some people realise their full potential while others get nowhere near it.

In one of her best-known experiments she presented a

class of students at the University of Hong Kong with an assignment full of challenging tasks. After the students had completed the assignment, one of the groups was praised for its efforts, while the other group was complimented on its intelligence. In subsequent tests, Carol Dweck observed an interesting pattern.

The children who were praised for their intelligence were distinctly passive and reluctant to carry out the most challenging assignments, and their test results got worse and worse, while the children praised for their effort kept improving. Next she asked the students to write a letter to students at another school, describing their perceptions and experiences of the tests they had undergone.

When she read the letters, she discovered something surprising. Forty per cent of the students who were praised for their intelligence had lied about their results in the tests. They claimed that their test results were better than they actually were. As Carol Dweck put it: 'We took ordinary students and turned them into liars by praising them for their intelligence.'

In a subsequent experiment, Dweck offered the students an extra course that would improve their language squeals. One would expect most students to show some interest because all classes at the University of Hong Kong are conducted in English, so it is almost impossible to do well without a decent grasp of the language. It transpired, however, that the majority of the students who had been praised for their intelligence preferred to stay at home and abandon the course. As Dweck explained: 'They care so much about looking smart that they act dumb, for what could be dumber than giving up a chance to learn something that is essential for your own success?'

These students were not normally deceitful; neither were they less intelligent or less self-confident than the other students. This study shows what happens when people end up in an environment that exclusively celebrates their natural talent and not, say, their commitment and application. They begin to define themselves by that talent-description, and when times get tough and that self-image is threatened, they have difficulty dealing with the consequences, to the point that they would rather lie than be exposed as untalented.

It's easy to see how this study might cast light on the mystery of Freddy Adu's failure. Remember what the legendary Pelé said to him when he was twelve years old – 'Listen here, God has given you the gift to play football.' Was Freddy being praised for his efforts and his work, or for his natural talent? The parallels with the children in Dweck's experiments who were praised for their intelligence, are obvious. It seems very possible that Freddy Adu became – and probably still is – hostage to a talent-description that was bestowed upon him when he was ten years old.

The child prodigy problem

Freddy's story is not the only one of its kind, by any means. This phenomenon is widely known as the child prodigy problem. The whole issue of so-called child prodigies and why they rarely achieve the success everyone expects is familiar in many fields and industries. It's often not the people who start out the best that end up the best – they seem to hit some kind of wall. As the former American president Calvin Coolidge has said: 'Nothing is more common than unsuccessful people with talent.'

But why should that be? Why don't prodigies succeed more often? Why don't kids who are the world's best at age 15 end up being the world's best at age 25? Perhaps being good too early can actually be a disadvantage. Perhaps people succeed in the long term more in spite of their early success than because of it.

Essentially, the child prodigy problem is to do with mindset; the difference between one which drives someone to move forward and one which causes them to stand still. Stephen Francis, Carol Dweck and Freddy Adu all have something to teach us here.

Francis consistently rejects athletes – either directly or by means of his less-than-impressive facilities – who are lionised, celebrated and honoured for their God-given talent. If sprinters tell a story of uninterrupted success, he becomes suspicious about their mindset. As he explains: 'In my experience, it is very difficult to work with people who have been too proficient too early. For one thing, they are not very open to new input, and for another, they have problems maintaining and developing their motivation. They seem to feel entitled to win.'

Child prodigies often experience these motivation problems. They don't like to work too hard (they generally haven't had to) and they tend to burn out easily. Think back to Carol Dweck's experiment: she not only observed deceitfulness among the children who had been praised for their intelligence, but she also noticed how they were drained of motivation. The talent-label made them think: why work hard if I was born with my abilities?

A major Swedish study dating from 1993 entitled 'The path to the national level in sports in Sweden' came to similar conclusions. A team of researchers took a closer look at the golden generation of Swedish tennis players, including Mats Wilander, Stefan Edberg, Joakim Nyström, Peter Lundgren and Anders Järryd, who all followed on the heels of the legend Björn Borg. Three of them ranked as number one in the world within a few years and together they harvested nine grand slam titles. However, the study showed that none of them had been among the absolute best youth players in Sweden. They may have been part of the elite, but they were not the very best. The study suggested that because they were never quite the best in their youth, always trying to catch up with those above them, they were more motivated to improve their game. They developed what Carol Dweck calls a growth mindset. Here, the driving force is not the need for social confirmation, but the drive to master skills, improve oneself, set new standards and do better today than you did yesterday. As Stephen Francis puts it: 'It occurs to me that people will last longer if they have not had too much success too early in their careers. I have seen how just a bit of success can cause major motivation problems. At the highest level, there is so little difference between people that if you're not extremely motivated you don't have a chance. I only want the ones that are really hungry, and often they don't have a long history of success behind them.'

It seems paradoxical, but perhaps a little failure is the key to success. Colm O'Connell seems to agree. 'A winner is a loser who has evaluated himself,' he says. Apparently there is something about having faced adversity early that helps to propel some people to greater success, and which continues to fuel their desire to improve themselves in spite of their achievement along the way. The hardiest plants survive harsh environments.

The cycle of complacency

The same psychological mechanism that killed Freddy Adu's promising career and caused the students at the University of Hong Kong to perform more poorly rears its head in business. Here there are countless examples of success leading to complacency, and complacency leading to failure.

We see this, for example, when major monopolies fall into disarray. The power of being in control of a monopoly makes companies become complacent, for why should they change a strategy and philosophy that has proven to be stronger than any other? The company stagnates, doing the same old thing, while competitors are forced to innovate in order to close the gap. When, through their efforts, these competitors suddenly overtake it, the original company finds itself foundering, crippled by a lack of enterprise and by the limits of its self-perception.

The cause of complacency is almost always success, or rather perceived success – it is not hard facts, but subjective perceptions of success that make the difference. As Professor John Kotter of Harvard Business School writes in his thought-provoking book *A Sense of Urgency*: 'With success comes a major problem: keeping up the sense of urgency needed to accomplish a bigger goal or to sustain a high level of performance over time.'

When people or organisations achieve some measure of success this naturally pushes them towards stability and contentment: 'At no time are these natural forces stronger than after people have worked very hard and have been rewarded by a visible, unambiguous win,' says Kotter.

Any executive who wants to create results and to keep on doing so should ask themselves: how do I avoid this complacency growing in me and the people around me? And how do I maintain *urgency* when we achieve success?

The typical pattern is simple: urgency leads to success leads to complacency. But this cycle needs to be broken, so that urgency leads to success leads to more urgency.

In his book *How the Mighty Fall* the American management guru Jim Collins describes how eleven renowned, successful companies have gone from success to failure, and how they learned of their impending demise far too late. Complacency sneaks its way into organisations like a cancer. As Jim Collins puts it: 'I've come to see institutional decline like a staged disease: harder to detect but easier to cure in the early stages, easier to detect but harder to cure in the later stages.'

The best way to combat complacency is to identify the symptoms in their infancy so that they are not allowed to develop into insoluble problems.

Here are four of the earliest symptoms of complacency:

1. People act as if they are too big to fail

Complacent people often view their success as 'deserved', rather than earned. They lose contact with the reasons for their success and begin to believe that it is their right. They are convinced that success will continue more or less regardless of what they do. They entirely underestimate the role good fortune and random circumstances may have played in their previous success, or perhaps forget that they did initially have to work hard for it. This cocktail of attitudes creates the kind of complacency that poisons potential.

The most typical consequence of this attitude is that people begin to take thoughtless or unwise risks in their quest for success – what Jim Collins calls an 'unsustainable quest for growth'. Success causes them to believe that they can walk on water; they feel immortal, too big to fail.

2. People look out the window before looking in the mirror

People who become complacent have a tendency to look in the mirror, taking credit themselves when things go well, and to look out of the window to blame other factors when things go wrong – or else go into denial. Jim Collins writes: 'Leaders discount negative data, amplify positive data, and put a positive spin on ambiguous data. Those in power start to blame external factors for setbacks rather than accept responsibility.'

Think back to Carol Dweck's study, where students lied about their results to sustain their perceived image of themselves as successful in the outside world. It was more important for them to look good than to improve themselves. That is the way it is with complacent people. They live in their own highly selective reality and often deny the facts. They would rather lie about their results than risk exposure as being devoid of innate talent. But as Carol Dweck writes: 'Why waste time proving over and over how great you are, when you could be getting better? Why hide deficiencies instead of overcoming them? And why avoid challenges, instead of looking at them as experiences that will stretch you?'

Any business executive, athlete, musician, singer or student gets confronted with situations in which they have to make the choice: do I want to look good, or do I want to get better?

The decisions we make when faced with such choices are crucial to our long-term success.

3. People are more inside-focused than outside-focused

When people start to pay more attention to what is happening internally than externally this is often symptomatic of a problem. They start to develop a feeling of contentment with the status quo. They sit tight. They focus on themselves and why they are great, and they ignore the hardworking competitors around them.

The same thing that happens to individuals can also occur in businesses. Instead of focusing on their customers, organisations develop a 'we know best' culture. They become sidetracked and start holding inconsequential meetings, discussing what colour they ought to paint the walls or whether they should hang more paintings in the canteen; they become hung up on the trappings of success and stop worrying about how to sustain their performance. The shift in attitude is clear: we are rich. We are the best. Let's relax, maybe grab a spot of lunch. It becomes more important to feel good than to do well.

4. People slip into automatic pilot

When people become complacent they often stop seeking new challenges. Their lack of urgency leads them to run on automatic pilot without considering how they can improve themselves. Two professors at INSEAD Business School in Paris, Luk Van Wassenhove and Kishore Sengupta, have called this phenomenon the 'Experience Trap'. Comprehensive research in numerous industries has shown that many people never really get better at what they do. People with considerable experience are often no better at their job than people with very little experience. In certain lines of work it's an even sadder situation – people's performance actually gets worse, the more experience they have. For instance, it has been shown that experienced doctors achieve lower scores in tests about medical knowledge than less experienced physicians. It also transpires that over time, GPs become less able to diagnose from cardiac sounds and X-ray images, and that accountants become less competent at analytical tasks as they become more experienced.

We find the same thing happening with drivers. Studies have shown that after twenty years' experience behind the wheel, people check their mirrors less frequently and brake much later than new drivers. Why? Because they are driving on automatic pilot.

The cause of the Experience Trap is almost always complacency and too much comfort. As Mette Nørgaard and Douglas Conant express it in their book *Touchpoints*: 'Maybe you have been in your job for a number of years. You are good at what you do, you are respected. You may have a boss who is neither too hard nor too soft, a job that is not too big and not too small, and expectations are not too hard or too soft. That's great – except that when people get too comfortable, they often become less vigilant. They stop foraging for new learning and lose their edge.'

That's exactly what complacency does. It mentally pensions people off. The instant you no longer critically evaluate what you do, your experience, however extensive, becomes useless. The moment you start going to work simply in order to work, or go to training simply in order to train, rather than to improve yourself, you invariably become less competent. Be cautious when somebody boasts that they have twenty years of experience – perhaps what they actually have is one year of experience which, because of their complacency, is nineteen years out of date.

Divine dissatisfaction

Preventing or dealing with complacency is difficult, but it can be done. And if you succeed, the rewards will be great. Executives, teachers, coaches, scientists and performers could all benefit from breaking the cycle of complacency and sustaining a constant desire to improve themselves. Carol Dweck calls this the *growth mindset*, John Kotter calls it *urgency*, the psychologist Ellen Winner calls it the *rage to master* and the famous dancer and choreographer Martha Graham once described it as a *divine dissatisfaction*. All are referring to the same thing – an unrest that will drive you forward and which makes you more alive than others.

It is this force that smoulders beneath the surface in the six Gold Mines. You can't see it with the naked eye but you can sense it. The excitement that vibrates in the air at a Korean youth golfing tournament. The intensity of a perfectly ordinary tennis training session for little girls in Moscow. The aggressiveness with which the young runners in Bekoji eat up the track every morning at six o'clock, and the determination in the eyes of the Brazilian boys in the São Paulo favela. Hunger to win, to improve; and a willingness to do whatever it takes.

The mercilessly tough competition situations many athletes find themselves in help to sustain urgency. Being the best is very, very hard. There will always be someone better than you. In Iten, for example, more than 800 athletes train three times a day. Competition between them is absurdly tough, forcing each to deliver their very best every single day. Every day you can feel the defiance emanating from your competitors and you know that just a couple of months of complacency can set you way back in the medal queue.

The same applies to an executive who wants to avoid complacency in the workplace. It is a question of dragging harsh reality into the organisation. Staff need to be able to feel the heat from dissatisfied customers, competent competitors and frank, expert analyses.

Constant, immediate feedback

In addition to this the Gold Mines have understood the crucial role of feedback to keep urgency high. One thing in particular surprised me during my visit to Kenya. Everybody trains with a group. Unlike in many places in Europe and the United States, running is not an individual sport there. Three times world champion in the 3,000-metre steeplechase, Moses Kiptanui told me: 'You will not make international top class if you train alone.'

According to Kiptanui, training in groups has numerous positive effects. If you always train alone you don't train hard enough. You need the others to put pressure on you when you are tired. On your bad days the group is there to drag you up, on your good days the group helps to force the absolute best out of you. But most of all, the group delivers the vital, performance-boosting feedback that every top performer needs. 'It's constant, immediate feedback,' says Kiptanui. 'You always know where you stand in relation to the others.'

The Gold Mines have plenty to teach businesses when it comes to effective feedback. Companies often make two classic mistakes when trying to build a feedback-rich culture. The first is not giving feedback often enough. At many companies, it comes in the form of an annual performance review. It's really hard to get better at something if you are only told how you are doing once a year. Think about Usain Bolt. His job happens to be getting from A to B as fast as possible. Now imagine if Bolt sprinted for an entire season and got feedback on his performance only once a year in a 45-minute meeting with his boss. That would be absurd.

The other mistake is that people tend to surround themselves with people who make them feel good rather than those who will help them improve. But why look for friends or partners who will just shore up your self-confidence temporarily, instead of ones who will challenge you to grow? If you really want to improve your performance, you must associate with people who you know will tell you the truth. Receiving such feedback can hurt, as many top performers will agree, but it is often one of the best things that can happen to you. Honest feedback is frequently like getting into a very hot bath. It scalds to begin with, but then you get used to it and begin to like it. Eventually you start thriving on it!

Don't downgrade yet

The conclusion of this chapter is not that companies have to turn down the heating, remove the paintings from their walls and generally downgrade their facilities in order to be the best. Nor am I saying that sports academies should dismantle their ultramodern training centres and train in rusty old sheds and on uneven grass tracks. The suggestion is not that Roger Federer will not be able to win his next grand slam if he stays at a luxury hotel.

But we must understand that creating world-class performance does not necessarily require world-class facilities. The world's best athletes in the main did not achieve recognition and success through living in comfort and being lauded for their abilities, but through ambitious striving for excellence. Colm O'Connell, who has played a seminal role in more than 25 world records, puts it like this: 'What lifts you from being a good athlete living well on your sport to one of the very best is no longer simply being motivated by money. Take Wilson Kipketer, the former 800 metres world record holder; he worked like crazy even after he had many wins and had earned lots of money. His driving ambition was to move the 800 metres race to a new level in terms of both performance and style. Another good example is Haile Gebrselassie [Ethiopian former world record holder in the marathon and the runner with the most middle and long distance wins in history]. Athletes like him are driven by a form of performance idealism.'

These words are strikingly similar to what Brigitte Foster-Hylton, the Jamaican world champion in the 100-metre hurdles, told me when I visited the MVP Track and Field Club: 'There are so many things I can improve. For instance, I am obsessed with making the perfect start, and I intend to set times that nobody can beat in the future. It is striving for perfection that drives me to work so very hard every day.'

THE GOLD MINE EFFECT

The main reason why we choose comfort rather than mastery is quite simply that it is easier and more agreeable in the short term. But too much comfort is the enemy of improvement. Research has shown that the brains of domesticated animals are 15–30 per cent smaller than those of their wild counterparts. In other words: if you want to thrive in a highly competitive environment, you need to stay a little wild.

True, learning can fun, exhilarating and gratifying, but it can also be daunting, exhausting and discouraging. In the words of K. Anders Ericsson, one of the world's leading researchers on developing expertise: 'If you are in a world where the status quo is acceptable you will not develop. If you want to get better you have to make a huge effort. Improvement never comes without a cost.'

World-class performers commit to never-ending improvement. In 2001, while at his very best, Tiger Woods took time to break down his swing in order to rebuild it. He could easily have remained hugely successful by continuing exactly as he had been, but he chose to take one step backwards to give himself the opportunity of perhaps taking two steps forward. Despite his enormous success he remained a student of his game.

Making a commitment to mastery is making a commitment to a journey that never ends. In his book *Drive*, Dan Pink uses an asymptote to explain the nature of mastery. In analytic geometry, an **asymptote** of a curve is a line where the distance between curve and line approaches zero as they tend to infinity. However, despite coming infinitesimally close, the two never quite touch.

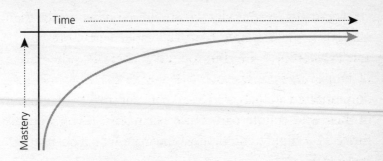

Pink writes: 'The mastery asymptote is a source of frustration. Why reach for something you can never fully attain? You can approach it. You can home in on it. You can get really, really close to it. But you can never touch it. But it's also a source of allure. Why not reach for it? The joy is in the pursuit more than the realisation. In the end, mastery attracts precisely because mastery eludes.'

This divine dissatisfaction is what characterises those who manage to avoid complacency and stay at the top of their field for year after year. In the words of Stephen Francis: 'The art of a successful mindset is to view your victories as a beginning and not as a conclusion.

What you should never forget about MINDSET

1. Experience is often a weak predictor for performance. In fact, a lot of people tend to perform worse the more experience they get. They develop fixed ideas and only work inside their comfort zone. Sustainable high performance is built on curiosity and the willingness to challenge oneself. The key to improvement is not found inside your comfort zone.

2. Labelling people as super talents often fosters the wrong mindset. They become driven by looking good rather than getting better. They validate themselves from the outside-in and not from inside-out. Success often comes down to one choice: will I choose the path of social approbation, or will I choose the path to true mastery?

3. A performance environment should never be too comfortable. You must nurture a constant feeling of positive discomfort, in particularly the discomfort that comes from being stretched to the limit. If you don't create discomfort from the inside, I'll guarantee you that you'll soon be forced to experience discomfort from the outside – and it's going to feel much worse.

4. Perceived success makes people feel entitled. As a result they become complacent and lose urgency. Anyone with the ambition to deliver high performance again and again must understand that. Change and renewal shouldn't happen when it's necessary. It should happen whenever possible.

The Godfathers

'Effectiveness is inherently paradoxical. To be effective, a leader must possess attributes that are contradictory, even mutually exclusive.'

Paul Evans, Professor of Organisational Behaviour,

INSEAD

The first time I met Stephen Francis was at a hotel in Stockholm in 2009, in connection with the prestigious athletics meet, DN Galan. I had already heard of him – his name was on everybody's lips when the then-unknown Asafa Powell shifted the world 100 metres record from 9.78 seconds to 9.77 in 2005.

The story of Stephen Francis turning Powell's fortunes around is far from being an isolated incident. As we saw earlier, Francis 'collects' athletes who nobody else wants and transforms them into Olympic champions and world-record holders. This is why I was now standing in the reception of the Nordic Sea Hotel in Stockholm waiting for the man who, in terms of results, is undisputedly the world's most successful sprint coach.

Eventually I spot him coming down the stairs to reception. He is clad head to foot in black, from his shoes to

173

the shades balanced on his forehead. He looks a little like a hip hop gangster – he is only lacking the baggy jeans and gold chains. He mumbles a lot, and takes long breaks in the middle of sentences, giving the slightly unnerving impression that he is about to drop off to sleep. However, the longer I speak to him, the more insight and perspective surfaces, and by the time I leave the hotel an hour and a half later, I feel deeply enriched.

Two months later I am sitting in front of the television watching the 2009 World Championships in Athletics in Berlin. Before the event, people were sceptical that Stephen Francis's sprinters could repeat their massive success at the previous year's Olympics in Beijing. All doubt rapidly evaporates, however. In an out-of-this-world demonstration of power they win eleven medals, six of them gold.

But if we are to understand the secret behind the Jamaican Gold Mine of top sprinters we must first understand Stephen Francis and the way the thinks. I had the same experience in Korea, Kenya, Russia and Ethiopia. All have their own Stephen Francis; a person who, from behind the scenes, creates and sustains an environment in which people achieve extraordinary success.

Don't start with knowledge, start with interest

After I had met these people, the world's best coaches, it took me a while to find a way to describe them properly. I toyed with 'Master Coaches', 'backstage winners' and 'gold prospectors', but none of these phrases really captured what I had witnessed in the Gold Mines. They did not convey the enormous respect and admiration these coaches enjoy.

As the Jamaican sprinters' in-house psychologist Dr Aggrey Irons put it when describing Stephen Francis: 'He is not just an athletics coach. He is a father figure to them. But at the same time, he has a giant ego. He commands respect and loyalty, almost worship, from his people.'

I experienced much the same aura around Colm O'Connell in Iten. Even Olympic champions and world-record holders had a look of gratitude and respect in their eyes when their Irish mentor was mentioned.

It suddenly struck me that in reality, these people are much more than just coaches. They are Godfathers. Although all the Godfathers I met and observed during my travels were completely different personalities, at the same time they had a lot in common. All were totally committed to their role. They read, studied and experimented constantly in order to refresh their knowledge.

Another interesting common trait is that not one of them had practised the sport in which they had become so successful as a coach. Stephen Francis was a statistician, Colm O'Connell a geography teacher, Won Park an environmental activist and Sentayehu Eshetu a PE teacher with a passion for basketball, not running.

'I have noticed that those coaches who have been successful as practitioners tend to force on their athletes the things that worked for them,' Colm O'Connell explained to me. 'They say: "Train like me and you will win like me". They can't see the athlete for their own ego. But in reality things don't work like that. The game is not about you, it's about your athletes. As a coach you have to understand that what works for one athlete does not necessarily work for another.'

Stephen Francis said more or less the same thing: 'The

coaches who are themselves former athletes tend to over-generalise from their own experience. What did or did not work for them personally has become their only blueprint for success.'

High performance is not either/or

While I was staying in the various Gold Mines, I tried time after time to get these Godfathers to reveal their philosophies. I imagined that they possessed some kind of secret, some 'golden method' or 'three effective principles'. But every time I asked them to be precise about their philosophy, they just brushed me off, saying: 'I don't have one.'

'Each athlete faces an individual challenge. There is no formula. I certainly haven't found it,' Colm O'Connell told me. 'If you become too systematic you risk standardising them. Of course I have guidelines, but I try to avoid the systematic approach.'

This absence of a single, rigid philosophy is something that I encountered again and again. While many coaches fix on a particular way of doing things and believe they have found the one and only recipe for success, the Godfathers have quite the opposite approach – flexibility. For them, high performance is not a question of 'either/or' – it is 'both/and'. Sometimes they are sympathetic and willing to listen to their athletes, at other times they are unreasonably demanding and dictatorial. They are angels and devils at the same time. They are also enormously ambitious and set the bar sky-high for themselves and others. Their methods won't always make their athletes happy. But their results will.

Yet at the same time they are enormously unselfish.

Unlike many self-obsessed coaches, none of them has the desire or the need to steal the limelight.

'A good coach knows that it's not about him, it's about his athletes,' Sentayehu Eshetu told me several times during my visit to Bekoji.

The Godfathers thrive on their backstage role, constantly in tune with their athletes' development. The job, as Colm McConnell puts it, is to 'inhale more than you exhale'.

They demand ever greater effort and investment on the part of their athletes and can be impatient when they feel they are not delivering. And yet at other times they can be enormously patient when an athlete needs space for their potential to unfold naturally.

You could also call them the 'maybe' coaches – when I asked any of them about whether a particular athlete would be a superstar somewhere down the line they just shrugged their shoulders and said 'Maybe'.

This does seem a little strange, though. If these Godfathers are so good at what they do, why can they not see who is going to be a star in the future?

'I've seen enough to know that you never can be certain,' Colm O'Connell explained to me. 'You've got to be patient with people because they mature at very different speeds. My job is to remain open-minded and maintain my curiosity with respect to each of my athletes.'

Although the Godfathers were all very open-minded about their methods and prepared to be flexible according to the needs of individual athletes, at times this attitude could be overruled by intransigence if their demands were not met.

As Won Park explained: 'I will do anything for my

players so long as they stick to my rules. Rule number one is that you train from sunrise to sundown. After that you do physical training, mental training and all the other training that doesn't require light. It's all golf from the time you get up to the time you go to bed. If that's okay with you, you'll have no problems, but if you are not willing to invest the effort, I will kick you out. Simple as that.'

The Godfathers are complex personalities. They are inquisitive but resolute; ambitious but unselfish. They see the big picture but also focus on detail. They are impatient but in a strangely patient way. They are sympathetic but incredibly demanding. The time has now come to meet each of them in turn.

Colm O'Connell

The Godfather of the Kenyan Gold Mine

On 25 June 1976, fresh out of college, geography teacher Colm O'Connell landed in Kenya. He had been given a job at St Patrick's High School, a remote boys' school way up in the Kenyan Rift Valley. Had anybody told him back then that 40 years later he would be the coach of the world's best middle- and long-distance runners he would probably have laughed at them, before wandering off to find the nearest pub. Until he set foot in Kenya he had never even attended an athletics meet. Nevertheless, the truth is that, measured in terms of titles and medals, he is the world's most successful middle- and long-distance coach. Cast your eyes down the long list of Kenyan world record holders and Olympic champions and you will have difficulty finding an athlete who, at some time or other, has not been trained by 'Brother' O'Connell, as he is known. He is the undisputed Godfather of the Kenyan Gold Mine. Here he is what he told me when we chatted:

When I first landed in Kenya I knew nothing about running. In fact, my favourite sport was football. Even today, I'm an ardent Arsenal supporter.

I didn't bring any set ideas or training methods with me, and I therefore had no option but to listen to the athletes and develop close relationships with them. Although over the years I have built up a considerable technical knowledge of the sport, I still try to accept the athletes for who they are and the point where they are in their development.

There are many theories, training philosophies and general frameworks used in running, but it is my experience that these are not what make the difference. If you really want to help an athlete progress, you have to get close. It's the relationship between the coach and the athlete that is important. Several of my athletes live in my house. That's how I get to know them best.

Coaching is not as easy as people tend to believe. You have to be patient; understanding of the athletes. You have to defend them and stand by them, especially when good results are not forthcoming.

As a coach, I also have to look at the background of an athlete – their family, friends and the other people who are important in their life. I have to look at who is influencing the athlete. I have to coordinate that support system.

Good coaching is not about charisma. It's not anything magical or elusive. You have to set clear goals with your athletes, motivate them to work hard towards those goals and work relentlessly to accomplish them. It's a long, hard road.

I treat everybody differently. I worked complete differently with David Rudisha, who recently broke the 800 metres world record, than I did with Wilson Kipketer [the former holder of the 800 metres world record]. They are completely different personalities, which means that the greatest mistake I could make is to believe that they are both just 800 metre runners, and therefore need identical training.

One of the most important lessons I have learned is to keep an open mind about the possibilities and potentials of all athletes. Athletes start at many different levels of commitment, enthusiasm and performance, and the rates at which they develop vary just as much. That means you have to be very patient as a coach; very, very patient.

People talk a lot about training, but I speak to my athletes just as much about relaxation. Very few people fully realise how important relaxation is. If your brain is working while you 'relax' it means that you are not relaxing. You must forget yourself, the things that are stressing you out – and forget the next session.

The ability to relax is underestimated as a factor in the Kenyans' success. The Western world has become so hyped up, so demanding and stressful, that it can be difficult to find peace and quiet. The Kenyan lifestyle facilitates quality relaxation to a much higher degree.

I also talk more about losing than winning. This is not negative talk, far from it. I try to educate my runners about the realities of becoming an athlete, part of which is accepting defeat. This is something that they do with grace and humility in more cases than not. They know it is only one race; that another will follow. A winner to me is a loser who has evaluated himself.

Won Park

The Godfather of the Korean Gold Mine

Won Park was originally just a Korean English teacher. He then became interested in sustainability and decided to do a PhD in environmental policy and management. His studies led to him to Las Vegas, to participate in an international conference on the harmful effects of golf courses on the environment. However, he became so enamoured with the sport that he stopped fighting it and instead became a golf coach! Today he is one of the most successful in the world. He has coached players such as J.A. Shin (highest earner on the LPGA Tour in 2009), Eun Hee Ji (US Open Winner), Jae Eun Chung (gold medallist at the Asian games), as well as numerous other Korean elite players. This is what he had to say to me:

My players must abide by my rules, otherwise I will kick them out. That means training from when you get up to when you go to bed. Some players may be lucky enough to get a day off a week, but most of them don't take their breaks. They train all year round, non-stop.

I use various methods to motivate people. For example, my players must pay two dollars if they go over par. All the money goes into a pool which goes to the winning player.

The first time I stood on a golf course with an iron in my hand I thought it would be a piece of cake. I had read everything and I knew precisely what mistakes people usually make. But when I tried myself I found that my body refused to follow my head.

Concentrating on something for more than 30 minutes is impossible. It's part of human nature. Even 30 seconds is difficult. Try to focus on the tip of your finger for 30 seconds without thinking about anything else. That's how difficult it is to play golf. You need to put yourself in a state in which you shut out everything and are totally focused on the present.

Most Korean coaches are former players, and so they teach on the basis of their own experiences. It works, but only if your players have the same mindset as you. It's important to understand that what works for you doesn't necessarily work for someone else.

Coaches should spend much more time than they do on their own development. There is always room for improvement, and if you are going to remain useful and relevant to your players you have to progress as they do.

I love to collect cases and stories; evidence of what it takes to be among the best. I tell my players what Se Ri

Pak had to go through to get to the top. She was the first Korean to make it, and it wasn't easy. Everything was new to her: the hotels, language, the other contestants, all of it. But she stood her ground. Her example shows my players that what they want to do is possible if they don't lose faith. I have an archive of stories, sorted by subject. Some are about engendering faith, some about making sacrifices and others about self-motivation.

I often tell my players that they must surround themselves with the right people. Being with people with negative mindsets will make them develop a negative mindset themselves. Positive mindsets are contagious as well – if you want to be a good putter, then choose a putter as your best friend.

It is mindset that sorts the best from the next best. It is the ability to constantly set higher goals, to push yourself and to learn from your mistakes.

Let's say I have two players. One of them finds everything very easy. Regardless of what I ask him to do, he does it perfectly. His problem is that he is not dedicated enough to his training. The other player, in contrast, is not so quick to master new techniques but is dedicated. He lives like a monk and does everything he needs to do every single day. In the long term, I have most faith in the second guy.

Talent tends to get in the way of itself. My task with someone who seems to be a 'natural' is to try to change his mindset, because he is not hungry enough. For instance, I will take him out to the driving range where some of the world's best players are training. I ask him to stand and observe them and write down a list of the players who arrive first in the morning and those stay longest in the evening. Then later, when I show him the top of the world ranking list he realises that there is an unmistakable correlation.

Sentayehu Eshetu

The Godfather of the Ethiopian Gold Mine

Sentayehu Eshetu has a whole list of Olympic gold medallists on his CV even though he has never been outside Ethiopia. Since he arrived in Bekoji 30 years ago he has been training the little village's children at six every morning on a track he built with his bare hands. He is famous for his insanely tough training sessions which push the children to their limits. Four gold medals at the Beijing Olympics can be traced straight back to Eshetu. These days, he is a celebrity among Bekoji's 30,000 inhabitants. Here is what he told me:

My dream was to become a professional footballer, but when I finished my teacher training the government sent me to Bekoji to be a sports teacher. There was nothing here. No facilities whatsoever. I decided to build a track for my students myself.

Derartu Tulu was one of my first students. She left all the boys way behind as a thirteen year old, and a couple of years later she was discovered by the Ethiopian Athletic Federation. When I saw how successful she was out there in the world, I thought: 'If I can do this with her then can I do the same with others?'

I have 300 children and youngsters who come here every morning at six o'clock to train with me. It can be difficult to organise training for so many people, but fortunately I have recently been given an assistant coach by the Federation.

My training methods do not come from things I read in books. I'm self-made. I have learned everything by trying things out to see what works.

These kids are willing to do anything to succeed, and I train them ruthlessly. That said, I have reduced the intensity of the sessions very slightly after one of the boys started to pass blood in his urine after training.

In Bekoji, people focus on only one thing. Running is business here. They focus on nothing else from the age of thirteen. They do nothing but sleep, eat and train all year round. I don't think they're as disciplined in Kenya, but then I've never been there myself.

My athletes' greatest fear is not getting discovered. They know that they have to go on to Addis Ababa if they are to have a chance of getting onto the world scene.

People in Bekoji are poor, but happy. They try to be thankful for every day. Even if they get nothing to eat they thank God for giving them another day to live.

The new Derartu Tulu [double gold medallist from Bekoji] is called Meseret Tadesse. I found her living with her family about 15 km from Bekoji. They were extremely poor. It took some convincing to get them to release her from work on the farm. They felt that they were losing valuable hands, but I told them she would be a better investment for them as a runner. Today she lives in a rented mud hut in Bekoji.

The only way you can get away from Bekoji is to be a good runner. It is impossible for young people to get an education that can advance them, which is why they commit everything to running. It's their only option. I've never seen anybody come to training late. They really want to do this, and they have no plan B.

Role models are the most important thing. The Bekele brothers and Dibaba sisters show all the children in Bekoji what they can become if they work hard. We need champions if we are to build the world's best athletes.

A lot of people in Bekoji get good at running because, when all is said and done, there is nothing else for them to do. Life here offers very few choices or opportunities. Running gives people's lives meaning and purpose.

I would like to start training marathon runners here, but I would need a bicycle to follow them across the terrain. A bicycle costs 100 dollars and I can't afford that.

Parents come here every week knocking on my door to ask if I will train their sons and daughters. They have seen what a running career can lead to.

Competition among the athletes is very important. It is very difficult to be the best in Bekoji; there is invariably somebody better than you. This means that everybody maintains their humility.

I remember watching the World Championships in Osaka. Dibaba stumbled at the start of the 10,000 metres and fell way behind, but she won all the same. That is the kind of survival mentality you find here in Bekoji.

Believing in yourself costs nothing. My athletes may not have the best shoes and the best training track, but they believe they can win. Sometimes adults over 40 ask if they can train with us. They still believe that they have a chance.

Stephen Francis

The Godfather of the Jamaican Gold Mine

A former financial analyst, for the last five years Stephen Francis has without doubt been the world's most successful sprint coach in terms of medals. Others in the athletics world have described him as pompous, arrogant and self-assertive, but he is known by his own athletes as perceptive and tremendously intelligent. As reigning 100 metre hurdles world champion Brigitte Foster-Hylton said: 'Every day I'm surprised how much depth there is in his outlook.' Here is what he had to say when we met:

Athletics is an individual sport, and many people believe that they can do things on their own initiative. I wanted to create a team environment, more like those you find in football. A footballer doesn't decide on his own initiative that he's going to train at ten o'clock. No, the coach decides that the whole team is going to train at nine o'clock, so that's when everybody turns out. I felt there was a need for a disciplined team environment in which everybody was in the same situation, regardless of their ability. I often asked them to start training at five or six in the morning.

I also raised the level of ambition. Among other things, I began to plan training sessions on Christmas Eve and on days when the athletes would normally have had time off. I told them that sprinters who win the World Championships and the Olympics don't take time off at Christmas. I wanted them to understand that they were not competing against runners from Jamaica. They were competing against the whole world. Our ambition was not local, it was global.

I don't recruit superstars with huge egos. Instead, I look for those with the greatest potential to develop. To begin with, nobody believed that the runners I took under my wing were any good. But I proved them wrong.

I sometimes tell my athletes that they know they are getting it right when for 80 per cent of the time they wish they were somewhere else. If you enjoy your job too much, you're not working hard enough.

It was easy to get my athletes to work hard actually, because most of them hadn't achieved that much. They were hungry. I would venture that it would be more difficult to motivate a person who had already run the 100 metres in 9.90. When a runner succeeds in doing something, he associates his success with his approach to the sport to date, and so it will be difficult to convince him that he needs to do something radically different. But a man who runs the distance in 10.6 or 10.7 is a different animal. So long as he believes you can help him, he will be willing to do anything you say. I wanted to change the way people trained and thought, and this was easier to achieve with athletes who had not yet seriously performed.

Conventional wisdom would have it that the greatest potential can be delivered if the coach has the opportunity to concentrate on the performance of a single athlete. The larger the training group, the less attention is available to each individual. I don't believe that is true. I have seen countless examples of coaches who only have one athlete to concentrate on, where that athlete does not perform at all well when it counts. My approach is to have individual focus but to train in a large group.

It is very difficult to see who will make it. That is why I take in so many athletes. I have more than 80 athletes in my group today, all training at the same time, and all of them are at extremely different levels. I've got guys who run the 100 metres in 11.5 seconds, and I have some who run it in 9.7. I have girls who run the 400 metres in 64 seconds and others who do it in 49 seconds. But there's no guarantee that an athlete will have what it takes to raise themselves up to the next level, and that's what makes the numbers so important. Right now one guy does the 100 metres in 10.11. When he came to me he ran it in 11.2.

If I hadn't taken so many in, athletes like Asafa Powell and Shelly-Ann Fraser might never have been discovered. Experience has shown me that many athletes do not mature for some time and that it is important not to shut the door on them. This means you have to be willing to invest your time and resources in something that looks rather ordinary but which in time can flourish to become something extraordinary.

Not many people in Europe believe that they can sprint, and this becomes a self-fulfilling prophecy. It's not because they can't, they had just been led to believe that they can't do it.

It's just like in war. Two sides might have the same equipment, but only one will win. It will be the side with the best trained soldiers. That's the way it is with sprinting, too.

What you should never forget about GODFATHER LEADERSHIP

1. Leadership is *paradoxical* – a great leader must be able to build close relationships but be able to keep at a suitable distance. They must lead from the front and yet hold themselves in the background. They must be in control at all times but trust their people and be willing to relinquish some of that control to them. They must be visionary but keep their feet on the ground. They must create consensus but be willing to make decisions against the majority if necessary. To truly become a great leader, you must recognise and reconcile these opposing behaviours. Godfathers master these paradoxes and understand that it's never a question of either/or. It's both/and.

2. Leadership is *situational*. No leadership style is universal. No leadership style works in all situations. Contexts shift and relationships change over time, and therefore great leaders are flexible. Bad leaders are static. The only tool they have is a hammer and therefore they tend to see every problem as a nail. The Godfathers use different leadership styles depending on the situation and the people they are leading. They don't please through their methods and philosophies. They please through their results.

3. Leadership is *relational*. It's the business of human nature. A hydroelectric engineer must have an understanding of the nature of water in order to build a dam. A physiotherapist must understand anatomy to treat their patients. In the same way, a leader must understand human nature in order to lead effectively. Godfathers have a deep insight into the psychology of people and understand what it takes to maximise their unique potential.

Not pushing your kids is irresponsible

'People say that you shouldn't push your children. But I feel the opposite. If you are not going to help your children to unfold their potential, then who is? I saw tremendous potential in my son and I didn't want to see him waste it.'

Enzo Calzaghe, father of boxer Joe Calzaghe

Does the name Elena Makarova ring a bell?

I wouldn't be at all surprised it doesn't. In 1995 Elena Makarova was the only Russian tennis player on the world women's top 100. At the pinnacle of her career she was ranked number 36 in the doubles and 42 in the singles with 547.80 points. That's a good deal fewer than German big gun Steffi Graf, who held first place with 4,592.86 points.

Ten years later.

On 5 June 2004 at the legendary French tennis stadium Roland Garros in Paris, two Russians, Anastasia Myskina and Elena Dementieva, were in the midst of a battle that would decide the winner of that year's French Open final. This semi-final marked the beginning of the Russian tennis revolution which would reach its climax three years later in 2007, when Russian women held half the placings in the world's top ten. This dominance has persisted, with Russia's share of players among the 100 best women oscillating between 15 and 30 per cent.

Elena Makarova has long since ceased to be exceptional. Wimbledon's courts are teeming with Russian players. As former world number one Serena Williams once said: 'Everyone on the tour is from Russia. Sometimes I think I'm from Russia, too.'

As I write, a fifth of the world's twenty best women tennis players are from Russia. The early twentieth-century poet Nikolay Nekrasov seems to have been right when he wrote: 'The Russian woman can stop a horse in full stride, she can walk into a burning house and at the same time she has the beauty of a queen.'

But the fact that in just fifteen years Russia has risen from being a nation unremarkable for its tennis-playing to a position at the top of international women's tennis is extraordinary. Although it is vast, the country does not seem much suited to fostering tennis stars – in most places facilities are decrepit, and there are more tennis courts in Paris alone than in the whole of Russia. Added to this the fact that the cruel Russian winter effectively prohibits all outdoor training for seven months of the year. Tennis players must fight to get their hands on the limited court time available at the few tennis halls. However, despite these atrocious conditions, the success of Russian women in world tennis is apparent for all to see.

By contrast, Britain, a once-proud tennis nation, has been reduced to the status of a mere wannabe. In the 2009 Wimbledon championship, nine out of the eleven British players were annihilated in the first round of the tournament. Those who thought it couldn't get worse were mistaken. In 2010 British players delivered their worst performance in Wimbledon's 135-year history. Only one home-grown player, Andy Murray, managed to make it to the second round. Home-grown is perhaps stretching it too far, as Murray had most of his tennis training in Spain. In 2011 things improved a little, with four British players fighting their way through the first round at Wimbledon. But with the exception of Murray, all got beaten in the second round once more.

This is not because the British lack ambition. Every year the government, sponsors and the Wimbledon organisation funnel around £60 million into the Lawn Tennis Association in the hope of creating winners. But despite this massive budget, which has equipped British future hopefuls with the best coaches, the best facilities and the biggest travel budgets, only two women and one man from the whole of Britain are ranked in the world's top 100.

All this begs a very obvious question: how have the Russians with their rundown facilities, an inhospitable climate and minimal financial backing managed to succeed while Britain, with what seems a perfect set up, goes from one flop to another?

Tennis as an escape route

'I can give you the politically correct answer or I can tell you the truth. Which would you like to hear?' asks Mikhail Ivanov with a serious look on his face.

We are sitting in the Russian spring sun at a cafe in the

popular Kitai Gorod quarter of Moscow. Formerly the home of the KGB's infamous headquarters, the Lubyanka, it is now full of fashionable shops and trendy nightclubs. Moscow is a city with two personalities. Half of it flashes a Western-style, cosmopolitan face, where money flows freely and the only limits are the ones you set yourself. But from the other half come stony looks and distrust; the result of decades of subjugation under a harsh dictatorship. This contrast has been obvious to me ever since my arrival in Moscow; it's a place where progress and stagnation exist side by side. One moment I'm standing outside a stylish club, the next I am walking past a grey concrete building where opponents of the Communist Party were executed en masse during the Soviet era. Many Russians stand with one foot in each of these worlds, and being aware of background proves crucial to understanding Russia's tennis success.

'Behind our most successful tennis players lies an enormous drive to earn money and escape from the material scarcity which they grew up under,' Mikhail Ivanov tells me, once I've said I'd like to hear the truth.

One of Russia's most respected tennis experts, Ivanov is now editor-in-chief of *Tennis Weekend* magazine. He tried to make a tennis star of his son and got him into a recognised tennis academy in France. But the food in France was 'too good', as he puts it – life became too comfortable and his son lost his appetite for success. Now 23, he is in Russia earning a bit of money as a tennis coach to help support himself while he studies.

'Take Maria Sharapova [three times grand slam winner], who came from a small village somewhere out in nowhere Siberia,' Ivanov says. 'Tennis was the only means she and

her father had of getting out of there. Or take Yevgeny
Kafelnikov [Olympic winner in Sydney and later number
one on the world ranking], whose father was a taxi driver
in Sochi, close to the border with Georgia. Tennis was his
only means of escape. I could go on.'

'Not one single player comes to mind who had rich parents and who made it to the top,' he continues. 'Many of
our top players come from shitholes outside Moscow where
there is neither infrastructure nor educational opportunities. It's not quite the end of the world, but you can see the
end of the world from there. Tennis is a means of escape.'

The Russian players' hungriness to escape their circumstances makes good sense to me. But it still doesn't explain
why in the last ten years the country has suddenly gone
from having one single player in the top 100 world female
tennis players to occupying more than 20 per cent of the
list. After all, Russia must always have had ambitous tennis
players with the potential to join the world elite, but never
before has this manifested itself with the dramatic results we
have now witnessed. I ponder this as I leave Mikhail Ivanov
at the Kitai Gorod cafe. Something must have opened the
floodgates for the hungry Russian players. A couple of days
later I realise that the answer is to be found in the depths of
the Russian political system.

A Molotov cocktail of pent-up ambitions

In 1997, on a packed Centre Court at Wimbledon, the
sixteen-year-old Russian Anna Kournikova caused a sensa-
tion by playing her way to the semi-final after defeating the
world number ten, German Anke Huber.

True, she did lose the following day's semi-final to the

THE GOLD MINE EFFECT

hottest star of the time, Martina Hingis, and later faded out, attracting more attention in fashion magazines than on the tennis courts, but her victory at Wimbledon proved to be the first in a Russian shake-up which would entirely change the anatomy of the world league table.

The seeds for Kournikova's breakthrough were planted several years earlier, and by an unlikely gardener. Boris Yeltsin loved tennis. He started playing to combat stress, appointing the head of the Russian Tennis Federation Shamil Tarpishev as his personal coach and doubles partner. And while he was in office from 1991 to 1999, images of the tennis-playing president were often shown on television.

However, Yeltsin was not simply interested in tennis for himself, he was also a genuine connoisseur of the sport. He was deeply engaged in the cause of professionalising Russian tennis and often conversed face-to-face with Russia's best players. He initiated substantial funding for facilities, coaches and travel budgets for the Russian Tennis Federation. In 1990 there were fewer than 200 tennis courts in Russian; today there are 2,500. Fifteen years ago there were 120 annual tournaments and today there are more than 1,000. In this way, Yeltsin both popularised tennis and gave people more opportunity to play it. It became a game for Russia's VIPs. Foreign Minister Andrey Kozyrev played, as did Defence Minister Igor Sergeyev, and the country's hotshot businessmen made many important deals over tennis matches. Even today, Moscow has tennis tournaments for businessmen which cost up to 2,500 dollars simply to participate.

Without realising it, Yeltsin opened the doors to a Russian Gold Mine. At the same time, the collapse of communism meant that tennis players no longer had to hand over their winnings to the state, greatly increasing the incentive to win. People had been given their passports back, so tennis players could leave the country. At last Russian players had the freedom and incentive to allow them to take to the world stage.

Kournikova was the first Russian woman to take advantage of this. She left for Nick Bolettieri's tennis academy in Miami at the tender age of ten, and other child stars followed in her wake. As the former top player and coach at Spartak, Olga Morozova explained to me: 'As soon as Anna Kournikova's mother had raised the money to send her daughter abroad, all the other parents worked like crazy to find sponsors so that their daughters could follow suit.'

Kournikova became the first female tennis millionaire, New Russia's first sex symbol and the first to enjoy the good life. While the gorgeous Russian dated Hollywood stars, her compatriots and their parents slogged hard to become next in the queue, all eager to taste the glamour, the fame and the money that went with success in world tennis. The tennis iron curtain had fallen!

Next in the Russian pipeline

Three hours' drive from the bustle of Moscow lies Kaluka. As my driver said before I got out of the car: 'If you need to go to the toilet, do it now, because you shouldn't expect to see a toilet for the next three hours.'

Kaluka has absolutely no tradition of producing good tennis players. Even today, there are only two shabby indoor courts and seven equally miserable outdoor courts for a population of 615,000. Even so, tennis is why I have come to this town. This is where eight-year-old Sabrina lives with her parents. In Moscow, they are already talking about her. She recently signed a contract with the management company responsible for superstars like Dinara Safina and Elena Dementieva.

I am met at Kaluka's town limits by Sabrina's father Oleg who is waiting for me at a lay-by in an old white Lada. He is wearing a tight white T-shirt and smoking a cigarette out of the window. Two years ago he took his then six-year-old daughter with him to play tennis. Just like other children she wasn't able to hit the ball to begin with, but even so he thought he saw potential in her. He reckoned that with his Master's degree in athletics he could get her into good shape. Then he would simply have to get hold of the right coaches to help him. Today, two years later, Sabrina is considered to be the best eight-year-old girl player in Russia.

We follow Oleg to one of Kaluka's few tennis courts. They are in a miserable state. There are huge holes in the asphalt and the net in the middle of one of the court is stretched between two rusty chairs. The concrete wall surrounding the courts has been sprayed all over with graffiti; in the clubhouse there is a dilapidated wooden hut. Oleg points to a little girl in a blue peaked cap running around one of the courts. It's Sabrina, and this is where she trains. She has just played her first tournament in Moscow. Oleg explains that she unfortunately lost the final, but then her opponent was two years older than her. He also believes there was some kind of conspiracy between the umpire and the opponent's coach, both of whom were from Moscow.

Today, Sabrina spars against a fifteen-year-old boy almost twice her size. As she effortlessly returns the boy's ground strokes, Oleg looks at me and smiles proudly. Sabrina and

The facilities at Kaluka tennis court are Spartan

her dad are very ambitious. They don't just want her to be number one in the world, they want her to win at least two grand slams.

'She set that goal herself when she was seven,' explains Oleg. She recently asked him if they could buy satellite TV

Sabrina playing on one of the court in Kaluka

so that she could watch more tennis channels. He didn't hesitate. Both Oleg and his wife Svetlana have PhDs in biology, but there is no work for them in Russia. They make ends meet by renting out fishing tackle. The good thing about that is that they can plan their own working hours – perfect when you are a full-time tennis parent.

'I have no other goals in my life,' says Oleg. 'My only goal is my child, so it is only natural for me to throw everything at her career.'

The hungry parents

Oleg's greatest inspiration is Piotr Wozniacki, the father of Danish-Polish Caroline Wozniacki, the world number one for nearly two consecutive years. Oleg read about how Piotr had systematically worked to develop his daughter's tennis skills from the age of five in a Russian tennis magazine. He recorded her training and evaluated her play every day. Oleg always has his video camera with him when he and Sabrina make the three and a half hour drive to Moscow to train with the best coaches. 'I film all the coaches' technical explanations and instructions so that I can learn from them myself and so be in a better position to help Sabrina,' he tells me.

In addition, Oleg has what he claims must be one of Russia's largest tennis libraries – a huge collection of books CDs, DVDs and professional magazines containing the stories of the most important figures in tennis on and off the court. He tries out all kinds of new ideas on the basis of his research. At one stage, inspired by something he read about reward systems, he set up ten targets on the courts in Kaluka, gave Sabrina 70 balls and promised her ten roubles every time she hit a target. He has stopped doing that now because it was getting far too expensive.

Oleg is aware that he is essential to his daughter's success. Last week he succeeded in securing Maria Sharapova's old coach's help in training Sabrina. He expects that within the next four to five years the family will move to Europe or the United States to train, just like Sharapova's, Safin's and Kournikova's. In fact, he already has his sights on German and French academies. 'We share this project and we are prepared to sacrifice everything,' Oleg tells me.

Sabrina with her father and mother, and the author

This attitude is not uncommon in Russia. There are thousands of ambitious parents who are willing to sacrifice everything for their children's success. As Mikhail Ivanov told me during our conversation in Moscow: 'Take away the parents, and you have no Russian tennis success story. In the US they describe the Williams sisters' father as extreme and perhaps even raving mad. In Russia that kind of parent is quite normal. There are always ambitious, fierce and goal-oriented parents behind our top players. Without her parents, Svetlana Kuznetsova would never have escaped from St Petersburg. Without her mother, Elena Dementieva would never have got anywhere near the level she is at today. The list is endless.' After my day trip to Kaluka, I return to Moscow and decide to spend the next couple of days testing Ivanov's conviction. It quickly transpires that he is right. Take a look at the following list of Russian players whose parents have been crucial to their success:

Player: Dinara Safina

Parents: Rauza Islanova, herself a former top player, and Mikhail Safin, manager of the Spartak Tennis Club, also a former athlete.

Parental influence: Rauza took responsibility for coaching Dinara until she was thirteen years old. Both Rauza and Mikhail then prepared the way for her to go to one of Spain's best tennis academies.

Player: Elena Dementieva

Parents: Viatcheslav and Vera, both tennis players.

Parental influence: Her parents tried in vain to get seven-year-old Elena into the Dynamo Sports Club and the Central Red Army Tennis Club. They eventually succeeded in getting her into the Spartak Tennis Club. Vera gave up her job as a teacher to dedicate herself 100 per cent to her daughter's tennis career. She has a reputation for controlling everything in Elena's life, from what she eats to who is allowed to speak to her.

Player: Svetlana Kuznetsova

Parents: Alexandr Kuznetsov coached six Russian Olympic cycling winners, and Galina Tsareva was six times world cycling champion and holder of twenty world records.

Parental influence: Because of her parents' great careers in the sport, Svetlana was first tried as a cyclist, although she was eventually allowed to choose tennis. One of her greatest strengths today is her endurance, which may in part be due to that early cycling training. Her parents followed her closely and got her into an academy in Spain at an early age.

Player: Vera Zvonareva

Parents: Igor Zvonarev, who played in the Russian bandy championships, and Natalya Bykova, Olympic bronze in 1980 in field hockey.

Parental influence: Vera's parents sent her to the Chaika sports club and found her one of the country's best coaches, with whom she still works closely to this day.

Player: Nadia Petrova

Parents: Victor Petrov, Russian hammer thrower and athletics coach. Nadia Ilina, bronze winner in the 400 metres team race at the 1976 Olympics.

Parental influence: Nadia was introduced to tennis at the age of eight and actively coached by her mother. Her mother travels with her around the world even today.

Player: Elena Vesnina

Parents: Sergey Vesnin and Irina Vesnina.

Parental influence: Elena was introduced to tennis by her mother at an early age. She is coached today by her father and the famous Russian coach, Boris Konuyushkov.

Player: Alisa Kleybanova

Parents: Mikhail Kleybanov and Natalia Kleybanova.

Parental influence: Alisa was introduced to tennis at the age of four and coached by her mother for the first nine years of her career. Her mother took her to trial coaching sessions at different academies in France, but eventually found a Romanian coach for her in Italy.

Player: Maria Sharapova

Parents: Yuri Sharapov and Elena Sharapova.

Parental influence: Maria was four when she started playing tennis. Her father, a former Siberian oil worker, took Maria to the United States when she was seven, without a penny in his pocket. He drove a taxi to make ends meet while trying to convince American coaches of his daughter's potential. He succeeded, and Maria was admitted to the Nick Bollettieri Tennis Academy in Miami.

Player: Anastasia Pavlyuchenkova

Parents: Sergey Pavlyuchenkov and Marina Pavlyuchenkova, both tennis coaches.

Parental influence: Anastasia's parents got her into an

academy in France at the age of sixteen. Today she is coached by her father Sergey, and her brother Aleksandr is her sparring partner. The entire family follow her around the world.

Player: Anna Kournikova

Parents: Sergei Kournikov, a Greco-Roman wrestler and professor at the University of Physical Culture and Sport in Moscow. Alla Kournikova, a 400-metre runner.

Parental influence: Anna's mother took her to the Spartak Tennis Club at the age of seven and to Nick Bollettieri's tennis academy when she was ten. Every week she pushed hard to secure extra coaching for Anna and worked behind the scenes to find sponsors.

Looking at this list it's pretty clear that the best Russian women tennis players have all been spurred on by fiercely ambitious parents. Anna Kournikova's mother inspired an entire generation of parents to make their children into tennis giants. All those parents had grown up during the Soviet era, unable to travel, to see the world or to earn serious money. That prison created a Molotov cocktail of pent-up ambition, which blazed up on the tennis courts. These parents drove their daughters to train incredibly hard at an early age, secured the best coaches for them and worked like crazy to raise the money that would give their girls a place at the best tennis academies in the world.

There are many contributing factors to the story of Russian tennis success but in the end it all seems to come down to those determined parents; their appetite and ambition. This not only explains the reason for the dominance of Russian girls in international tennis – it also gives us a clue as to the reason for the recent failure of British tennis.

Failure after failure

In 2009, Wimbledon, the world's most prestigious tennis tournament, was held for the 114th time.

In the stands sat the British Minister for Sport and Tourism, Gerry Sutcliffe. He had seen eight out of nine British tennis players crash out in the first round of Britain's own tournament and was 'embarrassed'.

He immediately ordered a post-mortem of the failure, demanding to know why the 60 million pounds worth of funding which the Lawn Tennis Association had been given had failed to produce results.

Sutcliffe's enquiries came to the obvious conclusion: in light of this massive financial support, unequalled anywhere else in the world, it ought to be possible to deliver significantly better results. Shortly afterwards things got even worse, when the British national team suffered a Davis Cup defeat to Lithuania.

Tensions had actually been building prior to this point. A few years earlier the Lawn Tennis Association suspended the funding of two of its best junior players, following them publishing pictures of themselves on the social network Bebo, eating junk food and washing it down with alcohol.

'Either they must behave like professional athletes or find something else to do. The sad thing is that I don't think they always understand the unique opportunity they have been given,' thundered the LTA's chief executive, Roger Draper, over the incident.

Various reasons have been offered for the ongoing fiasco

of British tennis. Back in the 70s and 80s, for example, the excuse for the lack of results was that the weather in Britain was not tennis-friendly; as soon as they got more indoor courts things would be different. But although the British now have plenty of indoor courts, the best facilities, some of the best coaches and certainly the best funding, they have still not succeeded in producing one single top player apart from Andy Murray. Why?

You can't buy your way to hunger

The LTA's National Tennis Centre is at Roehampton in south-west London. It is here that Britain's young tennis hopefuls train in state-of-the-art facilities. There are well-kept tennis courts and rows of treatment rooms providing everything from physiotherapy to dentistry. The corridors of the centre are full of young British tennis players dressed head to toe in Nike, with trendy Wilson bags full of rackets over their shoulders and iPods in their ears. The National Tennis Centre feels sleek and professional – it's not hard to imagine tennis superstars being groomed here. And yet, so far this hasn't been the case.

On one of the indoor courts behind the thoroughly modern fitness centre I find Olga Morozova, racket in hand. She is training a Russian boy and girl. Both have come to London with their mothers for the express purpose of receiving Morozova's prestigious coaching. Her matter-of-fact instructions and no-nonsense feedback fly across the net to the young players, who obey with alacrity. I have spoken to her many times on the phone during the last few months while studying the meteoric rise of Russian tennis. 'When you have been to Moscow and seen it with your own eyes come and visit me,' she kept telling me. 'But not before.'

Morozova is a Russian tennis legend. She was the first Russian to reach the singles final in a grand slam – in 1974 she made it to the finals of both Wimbledon and the French Open. After retiring from professional tennis in 1977 she became coach for the Soviet national team and then for the British junior team. Today she lives outside of London with her husband Victor Rubanova, formerly coach at the Spartak Tennis Club for, among others, Anna Kournikova.

'It has to do with hunger,' she says as we stand talking by the net. 'That is why the British players fail. They have no incentive to come to the fore, and you can't buy yourself hunger. Neither the British parents nor their children are ready to make the necessary sacrifices.'

And with all this available funding, the trappings of success seem to come to young British players too soon. They can have a great time travelling first class on the British 'tennis cruise' without really having had to work for that privilege.

Wimbledon legend Martina Navratilova gave a similar explanation recently in an interview: 'British players get coaching facilities served up on a silver plate without having to prove that they are willing to invest what it takes to become a champion.'

And four times grand slam winner Kim Clijsters said: 'You have the best facilities you can have here in England. Most of the girls who make it to the world elite never had such facilities when they were growing up. I don't think it's necessary at such a young age to spoil kids or to treat them like stars.'

The most successful British female tennis player is Elena

Baltacha. Not a particularly English name as I'm sure you can tell. She is actually from the Ukraine, where her father was a professional football player and later coach. The best British player over the last ten years, Andy Murray, has not had a typically British tennis upbringing. Apart from having had most of his tennis training in Spain, his mother – in almost Russian fashion – has always played a vital role in his career. Judy Murray has been heavily criticised in Britain for having pushed her two boys, Andy (number three in the world) and Jamie (Wimbledon mixed doubles winner) so hard. The fact is, however, that their performance shines brightly in the otherwise starless firmament of British tennis.

Judy Murray has also observed the lack of British hunger in the sport. She was recently quoted in several British newspapers saying: 'You occasionally see the British junior players out there on the big stages at the junior grand slams, and they look like deer caught in headlights. If that's the case, if you look scared to be out there, maybe you should be thinking about doing something else rather than playing tennis. In many ways, our kids are spoilt by the opportunities they have. We have to find a way to make them hungrier, to set goals which we then help them to achieve.'

Olga Morozova is now talking to the mothers of the two Russian players she has just been coaching. The mothers are avidly taking notes as Morozova explains the areas in which the children need to improve. One of the mothers gets a call on her mobile. It is the father calling from Russia to ask how his son did with his backhand.

'Of course, it has to come from the parents,' says Olga. 'It would never occur to any four-year-old child that they should train for their tennis five days a week. For example, we have an English friend whose son plays field hockey and is pretty good. One day I asked him why he didn't bring his son along to tennis. He hesitated for a moment before saying. "Yes, but I'll have to ask him first." "Ask him what?" I replied. "He's six years old."' Olga bursts out laughing.

'No, that's not the way to do it. You must present the game to him and inspire him to like it. That's your responsibility,' she says.

As far as Olga is concerned, everything depends on the parents' commitment.

'It's not enough for the child to have an appetite,' she says. 'It must apply to the whole family. I attach great importance to telling the parents what it takes, explaining why they must play with their children every day and get them to coaching five times a week. Being a tennis parent is tough, and there are masses of English parents who can't be bothered. They're lazy.'

I see evidence of this first hand at the second training session of the day. In contrast to the Russian tennis mothers, who show their children's training logs to the coach and discuss the day's programme, one English mother just sits on a bench reading a book. When I ask how she sees her role as a tennis mother she replies: 'I like to see that he enjoys playing tennis and try to encourage him as much as I can.' Ten seconds later she looks up from her book and says: 'But I hope they'll be finished soon so that I can get to the hairdresser.'

This is why Britain's development of tennis talent trails so far behind the Russians. We might look upon the single-minded commitment of the Russian parents as extreme, but there is no doubt that it achieves results. Their commitment; their willingness to invest time and energy in their children's careers far exceeds that of most British parents. Time and time again during my travels in the Gold Mines, passionate and ambitious parents turned out to be fundamental in fostering top performance.

Korea's golf dads

As with Russian and tennis, on the face of it South Korea doesn't seem like an ideal environment for people to master golf. In the winter, the climate is more reminiscent of Siberia than Florida. The green fees are the highest in the world, which you would have thought would scare most people off. And despite national interest in the sport there are still fewer than 200 eighteen-hole golf courses serving a population of 50 million. By way of comparison, Florida alone has more than 1,300 courses.

As usual we find a wealth of spurious explanations for the South Korean's success. Some people trot out the tired idea that South Koreans are born with special golfing genes. Others say that the country's history as a battlefield for superpowers (Japan, Russia and China) has built an over-whelming survival mentality into the South Koreans, while a third explanation is that after decades of needlework, Korean women have especially strong hands. The secret is much simpler than this. It comes down to the parent factor.

Korea is full of golf dads. One of the first things many fathers do with their daughters is take them to a golf course to test their skills. If they show potential, the fathers are ready to sacrifice everything. Just as Se Ri Pak inspired every one of the nation's girls to pursue a career in golf when she won the Rookie of the Year prize in her first season on the

LPGA Tour, her father Joon Chul Pak inspired an entire generation of parents to go for it lock, stock and barrel. He was a construction technician from the city of Daejeon. He had played amateur golf and when he caught a glimpse of potential in his eleven-year-old daughter he pulled out all the stops to make her the world's best. One of the stories most frequently told about him in South Korea is about how he dealt with Se Ri Pak's childhood fear of cemeteries. In order to put a stop to her phobia, he put up a tent in the local cemetery so that he and his daughter could spend time living among the gravestones. After dark he told her ghost stories until suddenly one night she said: 'I feel warm here.'

'Then I knew that she was strong enough. We packed up the tent together and never returned to the cemetery,' he said later. 'People said I was crazy, but I wanted to develop her self-confidence and toughness.'

Every day during my stay in Seoul I heard similarly incredible stories about how far South Korean parents are prepared to go for the sake of their children's golfing careers.

When she was nine years old Ha-Na Jang's father Chang Ho sold his furniture business in order to train his daughter full time. In 2009, aged seventeen, she became junior world champion. At that time, her father estimated that he had already spent a million dollars on her golf career.

Jiyai Shin was once number one on the world ranking list, but her path to success was far from easy. Her family always had to struggle to make ends meet and her mother was tragically killed in a traffic accident. Jiyai's father then decided to give up his job as a priest and become a golf dad. He drove Jiyai from one golf tournament to another in an old van, stopping at the cheapest motels he could find along the way. Today he is able to relax, lean back and say 'Mission accomplished.'

With their extreme dedication the South Korean parents seem to be balanced on a knife edge between madness and genius. Those who endorse them believe they are doing their children a huge service, while critics maintain that they are living out their own pent-up ambitions through their children, who are therefore never allowed to develop their independence or make their own choices.

But as Robin Symes, head of one of Seoul's golf academies, said to me: 'Far be it from me to judge what is right and what is wrong, but one thing is certain: if other countries want to match the South Korean women they need to take a good long look at what is going on here. There is no doubt that there are lessons to be learned from parents here.'

Choose the parents, not the kids

If you took the ambitious parents out of the overall equation, I am convinced that the production of top golf players in South Korea and top tennis players in Russia would grind to a halt. With their willingness to sacrifice everything for the success of their offspring, they have created these Gold Mines.

This makes perfect sense in the context of the other things we have learned about high performance. We have already seen that early starts are an ever-recurring theme in the stories of top performers. There is every indication that the training that you do consciously or subconsciously from between the ages of three and twelve has a decisive impact on the level of proficiency you will be able to attain in a given activity. And who holds the most influence over you at that age? Your parents, of course.

We must remember that adult life hems us in with many more obligations and responsibilities. Childhood is the period during which we have the most time at our disposal to develop and practise. It is certainly a time to be enjoyed, but it is also an ideal training period, an opportunity to build character and invest in the future.

The South Korean and Russian parents' methods may seem extreme and even draconian, but they are not wrong as far as one thing goes: if children are to become really good they must train an awful lot. Top performances are by their very nature something extraordinary. It therefore takes something extraordinary to create them, and in many cases part of the winning cocktail consists of ambitious and dedicated parental involvement.

A good example of this is Géza Szilvay, a Hungarian violin educationalist who founded the East Helsinki Music School in the 1970s. Here he taught 200 randomly chosen five-year-old children three or four times a week in a tumbledown old building in the Finnish capital. Today, more than 30 years later, 95 per cent of those children have become professional musicians and 5 per cent of them are highly proficient amateurs. Géza has continued to teach the violin, now at the East Helsinki Music Institute. The interesting thing is that the entry requirements for the course related not only to the children, but also to their parents. Géza interviews the parents of interested children, looks them straight in the eye and asks them a simple question: 'Are you willing to invest an hour to an hour and a half every day for the next five years teaching your child at home?' If the parents' reply is convincing, their child is admitted.

The implication is that, at least in Géza's mind, the parents and their commitment are a better indicator of a child's potential to become a successful musician than any of the qualities of the child themself.

It is not only in the tennis world, however, that we find ambitious, dedicated parents behind top performances. Even perceived geniuses like Tiger Woods, Picasso and Mozart had the backing of ambitious parents. As the American psychologist Ellen Winner concludes in her comprehensive study of talented children, *The Driving Parent*: 'No matter how gifted children may be, they do not develop their gifts without a parent or surrogate parent behind them, encouraging, stimulating, and pushing.'

You learn to love what you do

It stands to reason that no three-year-old child will volunteer to sit down and play the violin several times a day. The same applies to children who are singled out at the age of seven to become ballet dancers. I don't believe for one moment that all those children would go along with such a rigorous regimen on their own. No doubt many children end up in ballet schools because their parents had the dream of them becoming ballet dancers.

This parental ambition is vital – how else is a child to know what it takes to become good at something? And as we have seen, to really master something we need to spend at least 10,000 hours practising it. Left to their own devices a child might take a long time to discover what activities they feel really passionate about – or they might never. In either case all those valuable early years of practice time could be wasted.

A child cannot make the decision to become a top performer themselves. There is no way they can have any idea what they are letting themselves in for. But that is not the same as saying that children do not eventually share the ambitions which were initially their parents'. Many children come to enjoy the activities their parents chose for them because of the satisfaction inherent in mastering them.

They build up passion along the way or, as the South Korean golf coach Won Park puts it: 'You learn to love what you do.'

Ambitious parents definitely challenge the conviction that children should be able to choose what they want to do. In answer to my question as to who had decided that their daughters should play golf, the South Korean parents often pointed to themselves as though it were the most natural thing in the world.

As one of them said: 'If I don't push my children to play golf and hit balls for hours on end on the driving range they will never find out whether they can be good at it.'

A statement like this can be an enormous provocation to parents who believe that children should be given the freedom to pursue their passions. The problem is just that if you ask a child to do what he or she wants to, they may very well choose to go on Facebook or play on a games console for hours. The counter argument is that in the long run you cannot push your children to do something against their will. This may well be true, but I can still tell you one story after another about Russian tennis girls and South Korean golfing girls who, no matter how strict, insistent and demanding their parents were, are still dedicated to them and deeply grateful for the qualities they have instilled in them. There is no trace of bitterness or regret whatsoever. Even the girls who failed in their golfing careers despite huge investment on the part of their parents were thankful for what they had been given. One such person was Adio Jung, who I met in Seoul.

'Today I am the host of Korea's most popular golf television show,' she told me. 'The only reason I can do the job is because I know what the game is all about. And how is that? Because my parents pushed me to train for hours every day for many years.'

It's not always passion that fuels perseverance. Just as often it's the other way around – perseverance fuels passion. External motivators like family expectations and internal ones like passion often work together, in symbiosis. In other words: it's possible to do something because your parents say you should do it but to then gradually learn to love it.

The parenting dilemma

In 1985 the psychologist Benjamin S. Bloom carried out a comprehensive study of 120 men and women considered to be America's top performers in a range of disciplines – everything from swimming and tennis to mathematics, neurology and music.

Along the way, Bloom and his team discovered a number of distinct common traits in the immediate environments in which the performers had grown up.

For one thing, their homes appeared to have been extremely child-focused. The children were very important and their parents were willing to do a lot – almost anything, in fact – to help them.

It's interesting to reflect on. Perhaps the parents we refer to as ambitious are in reality simply those who get most involved with their children. And perhaps the worst parents are those who remain passive, perhaps in order to avoid responsibility.

As the successful tennis dad, Piotr Wozniacki, told me: 'The most important thing is that you have time for your child and that you invest in them.'

Another example is the Korean/American golf star Michelle Wie who charged her way into the world elite as a teenager. When her results began to wane after a fantastic rookie season, her South Korean parents were accused by the American media of being the reason for her decline – the suggestion was that they had pushed her too hard. However, nobody accused her parents of pushing her too hard while she was playing a fantastic game and earning millions of dollars during her rookie year.

It is here that we find the great dilemma in the discussion about parents pushing their children. On the one hand we might think that Michelle Wie's parents pushed their daughter too hard. On the other, we know in our heart of hearts that it was thanks to the many hours of training accrued in her youth that she became good enough to beat half the men in the qualifying round of a PGA Tour in January 2004.

Giftedness expert Ellen Winner of Boston College experienced precisely the same dilemma when she visited China in the late 1980s. She was 'flabbergasted' by an after-school programme in which first graders were required to choose an art form such as calligraphy or traditional ink and brush drawing which they were then required to continue practising for six years. In her book *Gifted Children: Myths and Realities* Winner describes how she asked a teacher:

'What happens if a child changes their mind or says that they didn't choose the right thing?' The teacher looked at her as if she was mad and said: 'That never happens.'

To begin with, Ellen Winner was appalled by the fact that children were expected to stick with something that had been thrust upon them at such an early age, but the more she thought about it the better she understood the logic behind it. As she explained: 'It was like an arranged marriage. But then I thought, "There's something really great about this, because these kids are really gaining mastery. And when they see that they're becoming good, they develop motivation."'

Back to Benjamin Bloom and his studies, which also showed that the parents of successful children greatly valued virtues like self-discipline and a strong work ethic. They tried to instil these qualities in their children – work before play, keep promises, keep pursuing your goals and so on. These qualities recurred in parents time and time again.

Rauza Islanova is a great figure in the Russian tennis parenting elite. First her son, Marat, became the number one male tennis player in the world, then her daughter did the same in women's tennis. As she told me when I visited her in Monaco: 'My kids know that I don't accept sloppiness. For instance, I don't hesitate to cancel a training session if they don't have water with them. That's poor preparation. To me, it's a question of engendering quality. It's not just a question of going out and training. You must think, and relate to what you are supposed to be doing. How can I win my game today? How do I win that next point? I have taught my kids to live and train quality-consciously.'

The parents in Bloom's study also played a key role when their children improved and needed greater challenges.

Children are frequently satisfied to be good at what they can already do. In that kind of situation it is largely the parents' responsibility to push the children out of their position of security so that they can continue to develop. At some stage the children in Bloom's study reached a level where they needed really competent teachers and coaches, which meant that their parents had to dedicate a lot of time, energy and (frequently) money in finding the right teacher and in driving their children to and from lessons or training. This is what Won Park calls 'shopping' – 'The good parent does his or her research and finds the best golfing coach in their area, the best physiotherapist and the best sparring partners, in exactly the same way as you look for the best doctor or the best dentist.'

On my visit to the Spartak tennis club in Moscow I heard repeated mention of Anna Kournikova's mother, who is a role model to other ambitious Russian parents. Although she didn't know much about tennis herself, she consistently pushed hard to secure her daughter the best conditions. As Katya Cherkasov, who trained with Anna Kournikova at Spartak, explained: 'Anna's mother always asked the coach if her daughter could have some extra coaching after the others had gone home. My parents never did.'

If you don't go to football training, we'll take you off the team

Benjamin Bloom's study shows that external factors can be extremely effective sources of motivation. Particularly in the early stages of taking up a discipline, children are dependent on this kind of external help; they need it if they are to stick with something and become really competent.

As coach Douglas Koh explained when I visited him at the Paradise Golf Academy in Seoul: 'To my mind there is no doubt that parental pressure is important when children are small. At that stage they are not able to motivate themselves. They need to be pushed. Then over time, they become less and less dependent on it.'

This is obvious even among the very best performers. Bloom noticed that their parents encourage them to train and from time to time they use threats and sanctions. However, the purpose of this pressure is to stimulate the child's intrinsic motivation. The parents Bloom observed did not say: 'If you don't practise the violin today you won't get any pocket money.' It would be something more along the lines of: 'Oh well, we'll sell the violin.' Nor did they say: 'If you don't go to football training today you'll be grounded all Saturday evening,' but more likely: 'Okay, then we'll take you off the team.'

The point is that if the child really didn't care whether or not they played the violin/football, the threats would have no effect.

This may all seem controversial and contrary to traditional principles of upbringing, particularly in the Western world. But we must remember that very few people will feel that an activity is fun if they do not feel they are good at it. And to get good at anything you have to work and push through obstacles, which is demanding and involves discomfort. It is in this kind of situation that young people need to encounter their parents as towers of strength who say: 'Perhaps you don't want to do such and such right now but you're going to do it anyway because it's important, and afterwards you'll be glad you did it.'

As Rauza Islanova puts it: 'If we agree that Marat is

going to go running a certain number of times to get into shape, then I expect him to do so. Even if it is suddenly no longer much fun, I don't let him off.'

Overriding children's preferences is important if they are to gain the self-confidence that is derived from feeling really good at something. In her controversial book *Battle Hymn of the Tiger Mother*, the Chinese mother Amy Chua writes: 'Western parents worry a lot about their children's self-esteem. But as a parent, one of the worst things you can do for your child's self-esteem is to allow them to give up. On the flip side, there is nothing better for building confidence than learning you can do something you thought you couldn't. My goal as a parent is to prepare my children for the future – not to make them like me all the time.'

Pushing your children has become taboo

Not many topics cause more controversy than parents who push their children, and people react in very different ways when I tell them about my observations in the Gold Mines. Some are angry, some are impressed and some nod their heads in recognition.

I often hear critics argue that for every Tiger Woods, Dinara Safina and Se Ri Pak, 1,000 other children with pacing parents never made the top but were devastated by the unremitting pressure to which they were subjected. Tennis has many stories of failure as well as of success – Steffi Graf, Mary Pierce and most recently Jelena Dokic all felt obliged to confront their fathers over the harsh training that they went through as children.

It is important to understand that not all pressure is the same. There are good ways to push people, and there are bad ways. In my experience, when things go wrong, it is invariably due to a misunderstanding of what constitutes helpful pressure. In Britain Judy Murray has taken a lot of stick for having pushed Andy and Jamie Murray to the top of their sport. But as Judy says: 'There is a big difference between people who push their kids to do things, and people who push to make things happen for their kids.'

All these sensationalised, negative stories have made a lot of parents reluctant. Pacing as a concept has become taboo. As a result parents wrap up their children up in cotton wool out of fear. They are known as helicopter parents, and serious cases as Black Hawk parents, after the American military helicopter of that name – they hover constantly over their children without giving them a sense of responsibility, discipline or consistency.

Some people are likely to be of the opinion that these South Korean and Russian parents are driven by frustrated ambitions of their own, while we are driven by family values and the love of our children. I'm not so sure that is right.

During all my journeys around the world I didn't comes across any cold, egocentric or callous parent-child relationships. On the contrary. They were close, warm and touching. This does not, of course, mean that there are no examples of the opposite – no doubt there are. But just because you push your kids doesn't mean that you are doing it for yourself and not for them. These parents are at least as driven by love of their offspring as non-pacing parents.

The main evidence is that much of what they do with their children is extremely demanding and exhausting. It is not easy for these parents to get their children to do something they don't always want to do. It is not easy to insist that they cannot miss training, or to convince them that they have abilities they did not know they had. And above all it is hardly pleasant to abandon some of their own career ambitions to focus on their children. In other words: it's not that pacing parents don't care about their children. It's just the opposite. They would give up anything for their children.

Much easier not to

Things tend to go wrong for parents when they pace their kids too hard and without love, or at the other extreme, with over-protectiveness and dishonesty. This second group are afraid to be too demanding of their children, and shield them from what they perceive as hurtful truths. This is the sad story behind the young people who appear on TV talent shows, only to be told by Simon Cowell what their parents never dared tell them: that their singing is awful and that they have a hell of long way to go to be anywhere near good. This kind of harsh truth can be devastating after a lifetime of being insulated from certain realities, and is the result of what is commonly called mistaken consideration. Furthermore, how can your children be certain that you're not lying when you praise them if you don't also tell them the truth when it is not so pleasant to hear?

As Rauza Islanova expresses it: 'I push my children all the time, and I'm really honest. "If you want to be good, you must do this or do that," I say. I don't threaten to kill them if they lose, but I do keep on asking them: "Why did you lose?" What was it that you didn't do well enough, and how can you train to solve that problem? I insist that they don't just accept their defeat but try to understand why they lost.'

Many parents act as though honesty will have a negative impact on their children's self-esteem. As the tiger mother, Amy Chua says: 'Parents frequently have conflicting feelings about achievement and try to persuade themselves that they're not disappointed about how their kids turned out. They worry about how their children will feel if they fail at something, and they constantly try to reassure their children about how good they are notwithstanding a mediocre performance on a test or at a recital. They assume fragility, not strength, and as a result they behave that way.'

We are modern, civilised people who want everything to run smoothly. However, becoming seriously good never happens smoothly. Conflicts arise, honest feedback is required and there is a marathon of hard work involved which, once in a while, will make you want to give up and do something else. Enzo Calzaghe, the father and coach of boxer Joe Calzaghe, told me this: 'Were there times during those 25 years when he'd had enough of me? Sure there were. And were there times when I was sick and tired of his ways and attitudes? You'd better believe it. But what brought us through was love and loyalty. It's just like a marriage. You don't survive 25 years of matrimony without fighting. But just because you fight, does that mean you have to get divorced? No, because the love is there. So long as there is love, you'll fight it through together. If you don't have a strong bond between you, one of you is going to bugger off as soon as you run into problems, as soon as the going gets tough.'

People who sceptically ask pacing parents the question 'Who are you really doing this for?' are often those who go to wine-tasting on Tuesdays and yoga classes on Thursdays while their children play tennis matches or practise the violin. They are often the same people who don't attend their son's football match on Tuesday evening because it's too cold, dark and rainy. Perhaps these parents are the ones who should be asking the question: 'Who are you really doing this for?'

What one has to understand is that pushing children in a constructive, helpful way demands time, commitment and persistence. Not bothering is much, much easier.

What you should never forget about PARENTING

1. Parents are often a better predictor for how their children might grow their potential than the children are themselves. Behind most top performers you'll find encouraging, stimulating and demanding parents.

2. There are different kinds of pressure. You can certainly push kids in bad ways, but you can also push them in good ways. I admit the balance is hard to find, but we often confuse egoistic and bullying parents with dedicated and engaged parents who are taking responsibility for establishing dreams and ambitions in their children.

3. The parents who criticise the idea of pushing children hard and who say they simply want their children to follow their hearts are often the same parents who go to wine-tasting on Tuesdays and yoga classes on Thursdays while their children are engaged in other activities.

Who wants it most

*'Champions aren't made in gyms. Champions are made from
something they have deep inside them. A desire, a dream, a vision.'*

Muhammad Ali

Not so long ago, most people had no idea who Shelly-Ann
Fraser was going to become. She was a middling high
school athlete – nothing to write home about. There was
every indication that she was just another Jamaican teenager without much of a future. One person wanted to
change this. Stephen Francis observed then eighteen-year-
old Shelly-Ann Fraser at a track meet just outside Kingston
and was convinced that he had seen the beginnings of true
greatness. Her times were not exactly impressive, but even
so, he sensed there was something trying to get out, something the other coaches had overlooked when they had
assessed her and found her lacking. He decided to offer
Shelly-Ann a place in his murderous training sessions. Their
collaboration quickly produced results, and a few years later
at Jamaica's Olympic trials in early 2008, Shelly-Ann Fraser,
who at that time only ranked number 70 in the world, sen-
sationally beat Jamaica's unchallenged queen of the sprint,
Veronica Campbell-Brown.

'Where did she come from?' asked an astonished sprinting world, before concluding that she must be one of those one-hit wonders that pops up from time to time, only to disappear again without trace. But Shelly-Ann Fraser was to prove that she was anything but a one-hit wonder. At the Beijing Olympics she shattered any doubts about her ability to perform consistently by becoming the first Jamaican woman ever to win the 100 metres Olympic gold. She did it again one year on at the World Championships in Berlin, becoming world champion with a time of 10.73 – the fourth fastest time ever.

In other words, the woman with the characteristic short, explosive sprinter's legs now jogging towards me across the MVP Track and Field Club's grass track after the morning's interval training is nothing less than a superstar. Shelly-Ann Fraser is a little woman with a big smile. Her accommodating, rather shy personality is reminiscent of an unconcerned college girl, but behind her childish enthusiasm you can also sense how serious she is. She has a mental toughness that did not come about by chance. Her journey to becoming the fastest woman on earth has been anything but smooth and effortless.

Shelly-Ann grew up in one of Jamaica's toughest inner-city communities known as Waterhouse, where she lived in a one-room tenement, sleeping four in a bed with her mum and two brothers.

'Waterhouse is one of the poorest communities in Jamaica. A really violent place, overpopulated, children having children, a lot of crime,' she explains as we sit and talk in the shade at the training ground.

Several of Shelly-Ann's friends and family were caught

up in the killings; one of her cousins was shot dead only a few streets away from where she lived.

Her mother Maxime, one of a family of fourteen, had been an athlete herself as a young girl but, like so many other girls in Waterhouse, had to stop when she became pregnant as a teenager with Shelly-Ann's oldest brother Omar. Maxime's early entry into the adult world with its obligations and responsibilities gave her the determination to ensure that her kids would not end up in Waterhouse's roundabout of poverty.

'My mother encouraged me a lot. I really love her because when nobody else was there, she always made sure to provide for us. It was hard for her; sometimes we didn't have enough to eat. I ran at the school championships barefooted because we couldn't afford shoes.'

It didn't take long for Shelly-Ann to realise that athletics could be her way out of Waterhouse. On a summer evening in Beijing in 2008, all those long, hard hours of work and dedication finally bore fruit. The barefoot kid who just a few years previously had had been living in poverty, surrounded by gangsters and violence, had written a new chapter in the history of athletics.

But her victory was far greater than that. The night she won Olympic gold in Beijing, the routine murders in Waterhouse – 30 in the previous seven months – and the drug wars in the neighbouring streets halted. The dark cloud above one of the world's toughest criminal neighbourhoods simply disappeared for a few days. As Shelly-Ann Fraser explained to the *Daily Mail* after her Olympic triumph: 'I didn't become just another Waterhouse statistic but someone who could uplift the community, who showed

THE GOLD MINE EFFECT

something good could come from anywhere in Jamaica – even the ghetto.'

Her significance as a role model for the people of Waterhouse made a deep impression on her. 'I have so much fire burning for my country,' she tells me.

She plans to start a foundation for underprivileged children and wants to build a community centre in Waterhouse. She hopes to inspire the Jamaicans to lay down their weapons. She intends to fight to make it a woman's as well as a man's world, and she is currently studying to become a child psychologist.

'When I go back to Waterhouse, I can see that I had a positive effect,' she says. 'It's more united, I see more kids going to school, taking part in sport. It makes me proud and gives me a lot of motivation.'

The difference that makes the difference

A couple of days after my meeting with Shelly-Ann Fraser, I am sitting with Glen Mills on a bench in the sun outside Queen's University in Kingston. He has just finished a training session with, among others, the phenomenal Usain Bolt and the new sprinting hope Yohan Blake.

In Jamaica, Glen Mills is known as the architect of Bolt's success. He is the man who resurrected him after he came last in the 200 metres at the 2005 Helsinki World Championships and was deemed a failure.

After this debacle, Bolt contacted Mills. The rest is history. Since then, Usain Bolt has toppled one world record after another, and has always attributed his extraordinary performance to Glen Mills.

Since my conversation with Shelly-Ann I have been

obsessed with what it is that actually makes the difference in the Olympic finals of the hundred metres. The sprinters know that they will only be a few hundredths of a second apart at the tape. A single blunder is enough to make the difference between coming in first or eighth. All will have been training like crazy to be fast enough. Motivation and concentration burn in the eyes of the sprinters as they place their feet on the blocks and prepare themselves for the crack of the starting pistol. In less than ten seconds it will all be over. But which factor, more than any other, determines who will be the winner?

I decided to put that question to Glen Mills. I expected a rather long, complex answer, perhaps something to do with a special sprinting technique, a superb start, a specific body type or something else along those lines. But he just looked me in the eye and said: 'Who wants it most.'

Do you have grit?

Motivation is the emotional foundation of all excellence, no matter who you are or what it is you are striving to achieve. As we know, it takes 10,000 hours, or about a decade of practice, to become highly successful in most endeavours, from managing a company to becoming a world-class sprinter. It takes powerful commitment, and the secret to success is often to want something badly enough. Jack Welch, the former CEO of General Electric, once said: 'Any company trying to compete … must figure out a way to engage the mind of every employee.'

When the Los Angeles Lakers suffered a crushing defeat last year at the Miami Heat in the American NBA league, the team's star player, Kobe Bryant, stayed behind for an

hour and a half at the stadium to train at the things he
had been dissatisfied with in his game. When asked why he
didn't go home like all the other members of his team, his
response to the NBA journalist Adrian Wojnarowski was to
quote the Greek hero Achilles in the film *Troy*: 'I want what
all men want, I just want it more.'

That's the way it is. If you want something badly enough
you don't have to worry about self-discipline and perseverance, they come to you naturally.

Countless researchers have endeavoured to solve the
motivation mystery and find the recipe to ths irresistible
drive, about which Glen Mills speaks and which Shelly-Ann
Fraser and Kobe Bryant personify.

One of the most interesting studies of motivation
was done by Angela Duckworth, Assistant Professor of
Psychology at the University of Pennsylvania. As a college student, Duckworth developed a particular interest in
neurobiology and became a teacher at a school for low-
income children. Here she began to wonder why many of
the children had reading skills that were four grade levels
below average. They neither appeared less intelligent nor
had lower IQs than other children. This mystery inspired
Duckworth to return to university for a PhD. She contacted Martin Seligman, the father of the modern positive
psychology movement, and together they began ground-
breaking work to identify high achievers in a whole series
of different fields, interviewing them and then describing
the characteristics that seemed to typify them. These top
performers were generally very different from each other,
but did all seem to hold one characteristic in common: a
determination to accomplish an ambitious, long-term goal
despite the inevitable obstacles. Duckworth and Seligman

noticed that people who accomplished great things usually combined a passion for a single mission with an unwa-
vering dedication to achieving that mission, whatever the
obstacles and however long it might take. Duckworth and
Seligman decided to name this quality 'grit'.

This is the same quality identified by the legendary
psychologist Lewis Terman in the 1930s, when he followed a group of gifted boys from childhood to middle
age. 'Persistence in the accomplishment of ends' was,
according to Terman, what primarily differentiated them
from less successful boys. More or less the same conclusion was drawn by Joseph Renzulli, director of the National
Research Center on the Gifted and Talented, where they
conducted one of the most widely cited studies of talent
ever performed. Renzulli emphasised perseverance, endurance and hard work – which he referred to collectively as
'task commitment' – as a crucial element of what we typically call giftedness.

The persistence and motivation Duckworth and
Seligman, Terman and Renzulli are talking about is a trait
common to all the greatest performers in history, even
among those who appear to have a gift that allows them to
excel with very little effort. One such person is Wolfgang
Amadeus Mozart. His diaries contain a frequently cited
passage in which he describes how an entire symphony
appeared in his head, in its entirety. But as Jonathan
Plucker, an educational psychologist at the University of
Indiana noted: 'No-one ever quotes the next paragraph,
where he talks about how he refined the work for months.'

Angela Duckworth and Martin Seligman have shown
in numerous contexts that grit is perhaps the best indicator of how well a student will manage in real-life academic

settings. But the importance of grit goes far beyond academic settings – it seems to be crucial even in the military, for example. Duckworth and Seligman demonstrated that grit was the best indicator when it came to predicting who would complete the first, extremely exhausting, summer training session (known as Beast Barracks) at the United States Military Academy at West Point. In 2008 they distributed a grit questionnaire to all of the 1,223 cadets entering the training programme. It transpired that those who scored the most points in the grit questionnaire were also the ones who survived the demanding first few weeks at the academy. Traditional indicators such as high school class rank, SAT scores, athletic experience and faculty appraisal scores paled into insignificance in comparison to grit. As Duckworth put it: 'Sticking with West Point doesn't have as much to do with how smart you are as your character and motivation does.'

The power of role models

So it seems clear that motivation is essential for top performance, but where does it come from? If we can understand that then it will surely be easier to develop and sustain it in ourselves and others. Two American psychologists attempted to trigger a motivation explosion and the results of their study certainly give us a lot to think about.

In 2008 Geoffrey Cohen from the University of Colorado and his colleague Gregory Walton selected a group of first-year students at Yale, who were asked to read an article. The article was written by a former student by the name of Nathan Jackson, and told how he had arrived at college without a clue as to what kind of career he wanted to pursue. During his studies, however, he developed a great liking for maths and after leaving college he made a brilliant career for himself in mathematics as a recognised expert.

In Nathan Jackson's story the students found a maths role model. However, Cohen and Walton had manipulated one aspect of the experiment.

At the bottom of the article they had inserted a small fact box with information about Jackson's home town, educational background and date of birth. In half the articles they had changed Jackson's date of birth to that of the student reading the document. The other half were given the article with Jackson's correct date of birth. Cohen and Walton asked the students to solve a challenging – in actual fact unsolvable – maths problem after they had read the article. The idea was to test the students' attitude and approach to the subject. How long and hard were they willing to work to solve an insoluble mathematical problem before they gave up?

All the students worked individually on the assignment and had no idea that they were being assessed. It turned out that the students who had read the article in which their date of birth matched that of Nathan Jackson showed a distinctly more positive and committed attitude to maths. They were persistent and worked 65 per cent longer on the unsolvable problem than their fellow students.

In other words: just because they shared the same date of birth as a maths expert they had read about, they were motivated to work harder. They didn't know Nathan Jackson and had never met him, but all the same he became a subconscious role model who kindled their appetite for maths.

As Cohen and Walton concluded: 'There is much to suggest that our motivation is kindled much less than we believe by our interests, passions or individual skills, but to a great extent by the social role models with whom we identify ourselves. People who connect with a role model become quite simply more motivated, even if they don't know the person concerned.'

In the light of this discovery, one might maintain that the earlier in life you meet a suitable role model, the greater the chance of you becoming motivated enough to train for the number of hours required to lead to elite performance.

With this in mind it will probably not surprise you that role models for the young athletes were in evidence in all of the six Gold Mines I visited.

They did it. Why can't you?

Every Jamaican has a picture etched in their minds of their countrywoman Deon Hemmings standing atop the rostrum at the 1996 Atlanta Olympics having won the women's 400 metres hurdles and set a new Olympic record. She was the first Jamaican woman ever to win an Olympic gold medal. During the victory ceremony, she stood with her hand on her heart as the Jamaican flag was raised above the Olympic Stadium in Atlanta and the Jamaican national anthem was played. At the moment it hit her what she had achieved, tears begin to roll down her cheeks.

The main reason for the familiarity of this scene in Jamaica is that the video of the victory ceremony was subsequently shown in every cinema in the country, where it is traditional for everybody to stand while the national anthem is played. In other words, you couldn't go to the cinema in Jamaica for eight years without seeing Deon Hemmings standing on the rostrum.

Back in 1996, Melanie Walker, Sherone Simpson and Shelly-Ann Fraser were little girls aged eleven, twelve and thirteen. They all went to the cinema with their parents and friends. On the big screen they repeatedly saw a perfect role model standing at the top of the Olympic rostrum in tears.

Just over ten years later, these three little girls, having grown up to become big stars, swept the competition off the track at the finals of the Beijing Olympics, to complete the 100 metres as numbers one, two and three.

I am not trying to saythat all you have to do is to throw weeping sports stars on the screen during prime time and then lean back and wait for Olympic gold medallists to spring up ten years later. But try to imagine what it does to children and young people when they are shown what they can become if they work hard enough – and what it means for their country if they do. Role models send a clear message: 'We did it. Why can't you?'

Deon Hemmings had exactly the same effect on young sprinters in Jamaica that Nathan Jackson had on the students at Yale. Role models are sparks that can light the fire of motivation.

In my experience, top performers are able to pinpoint extremely precisely the moment that they found inspiration and thought to themselves: 'That's what I want to be.'

As twice world champion hurdler Colin Jackson said in the BBC series *The Making of Me*: 'I can still remember my parents sitting in front of the television screaming, shouting at Don Quarrie [the Jamaican sprinter], cheering him on to win the Olympic gold in the 200 metres in 1976. I looked at them and thought: "I want to be just like him".'

Something similar happened to Ethiopian running legend Haile Gebrselassie. As a seven year old, he saw his countryman Miruts Yifter take the gold in both the 5,000 and the 10,000 metres at the 1980 Moscow Olympics. When he explained how that felt to me his words were almost identical to Colin Jackson's: 'I sat there thinking: "I want to be like him!"'

The Gold Mines are bursting with inspiring role models and cultural icons, who kindle motivation in entire generations. Spend some time in Jamaica, Ethiopia or Brazil and you will find that beneath the surface tiny seeds of motivation are constantly being planted. The High School Championships in Jamaica – the Champs for short – are a perfect example of this happening, and they made a deep impression on me.

The DNA of the sprinting powerhouse

Kingston, the National Stadium. More than 30,000 spectators are crammed in to the stands – it's a seething witches' cauldron of emotion. Weeks and months of pent-up expectation are finally being released. This is what the athletes from St Jago High School and the 120 other Jamaican schools have spent months training for. Down on the track the young runners are getting ready for the sprint of their lives. This is the stage onto which the 3,000 young Jamaican athletes march when they compete once a year for the title of king or queen in the High School Championships, which were held for the first time in 1910.

Which of these fifteen-year-old Jamaican girls and boys might, in a few years, take on the mantle of Jamaican sprinting success and beat yet more world records?

Next to the Olympics and the World Championships there is no event which obsesses the nation like this four-day competition. What sounds like an annual school sports day to the rest of the world is for Jamaicans the climax of the sporting year. It is so important that from the way Jamaicans talk you could be forgiven for thinking that it's matter of life or death. Tension builds for weeks leading up to the competition. The Champs completely monopolise the front pages of the newspapers and the top stories on the TV news.

During the competition, everybody in Kingston – from hotel porters and bus drivers to the fruit salesmen and the homeless – discusses athletics. Everybody has an opinion about who will be the next Usain Bolt or Shelly-Ann Fraser. Bars and restaurants install huge TV screens so that those who are not able to get into the stadium can watch live broadcasts. Viewing figures approach 1.2 million in a country with a population of 2.8 million.

Inside the stadium, every school demonstrates its support for its athletes with drumming, giant banners and loud cheering. Emotions run high and frequently end in violent clashes on the streets after dark, after the last race has been run.

All the celebrated Jamaican sprinters turn out at the stadium every year for the event where everything started for them. It is here that the stars are born. Bolt, Fraser and the others all talk about the Champs as the experience that defined them as runners on their way to the top. It is in this extremely competitive environment that the foundations of their mental strength were laid.

'It's the biggest thing there is. It's like the World Cup or the Olympics. It's extremely competitive, especially the relay race. The atmosphere of the stadium changes completely when the relay starts. If you are not strong enough mentally you crack up,' Usain Bolt said of his experiences in the Champs.

Or as five-times Olympic medallist Veronica Campbell-Brown put it: 'If you can perform in front of a Champs crowd you can perform anywhere. When a Jamaican athlete enters a stadium to face a crowd of 80,000 people it's just another day at the office.'

The Champs is the heart of Jamaica's sprinting culture and the intensity there makes an American track meet resemble any old training session. In the United States, friends, family and a couple of coaches will be in attendance. At the Champs there are 30,000 spectators. As Glen Mills told me: 'If you have what it takes to win the Champs and receive an ovation on the rostrum, you will do anything to get back up there again. It's a feeling you will chase forever.'

The Champs is an event that lights a fire in the bellies of future super-sprinters. It's an explosive cocktail of inspiring role models; ruthless competition that forces the best out of you; massive pressure that tests your psyche; and an adrenaline kick that you will want to chase for ever. If Martin Seligman and Angela Duckworth had been sitting in with me in the stands of the National Stadium in Kingston, they would see that the Champs are the perfect environment in which to develop grit. They demand rock-solid persistence and encourage people to raise the bar and perform at a higher level than they would have thought possible.

This happened for Yohan Blake, the current 100 metre world champion and holder of the second fastest time ever in the 200 metres. Blake attended St Jago High School

– one of the schools which consistently performs well at the Champs. Apart from Yohan Blake, the school has hatched world stars such as Melanie Walker (Olympic gold medallist in the 400 metre hurdles) and Kerron Stewart (Olympic silver medallist in the 100 metres sprint). During my visit to Jamaica, head coach Danny Hawthorne showed me round St Jago High School. He pointed out the wall of the stands in the school's athletic grounds. Somebody had written across it in white paint: '9.98 secs. Oh My God.'

The wall Yohan Blake painted with this goal

'That was written by Yohan Blake when he was eighteen years old and training with me for Champs,' Danny Hawthorne told me with a smile. 'His great aim was to run under ten seconds and one year later he did it. He wrote it on the wall so that everybody could see it.'

'If people want to understand what drives these girls and boys they must come to the Champs.'

Pure love of the game is not enough

Attempts to find out exactly what drives great performances have always revolved around looking at two factors: intrinsic motivation and extrinsic motivation. The question is, do top performers feel driven by their activity itself and the process of taking part in it, or are they driven by the rewards they can gain from it, such as prestige and money?

Most studies have concluded that the grit and persistence which characterise top performers stem from intrinsic factors. Pure passion and love are what have driven the world's best to break records. How would anyone otherwise be able to push through the years of long, difficult hours of training necessary to become world class?

We love that explanation, just as we love the sappy, romantic ending of a sentimental movie. My conclusion from studying the six Gold Mines, however, is that intrinsic factors are far from adequate when it comes to explaining the hunger that drives top performers.

Just look at 43-year-old Esther Kiplagat, one of Kenya's best female marathon runners. Throughout her childhood she trained extremely hard, running more than 100 kilometres a week. But after she retired in her late thirties she as good as stopped running. Today she doesn't go jogging on the paths around Iten or spend time in the gym to stay in shape. She is now an overweight woman in her mid-forties, and her story is far from unique in Kenya. If Esther Kiplagat really loved running, why hasn't she gone for a single jog since she retired?

Extrinsic factors play a far greater role than we are generally willing to admit. No matter how much we like to hear it, pure love of the sport is simply is not enough to carry you through to achieve world-class performance. The world's best long-distance runners, tennis players, golfers, sprinters and footballers hunger for much more than the self-contained fascinations of their sport.

Think back to three-times world steeplechase champion Moses Kiptanui. He had a far greater passion for football than for athletics, but because he could earn more money and help his family by running, he started training like crazy. As Toby Tanser writes in *More Fire*: 'The lure of prize money is powerful: a teacher in rural Kenya can make a salary of 4,000 shillings a year (approximately 580 dollars). The second finisher at a recent marathon in Huntsville, Alabama, won 750 US dollars in a time slower than the women's marathon group in Iten clocks on their training routes.'

Today, even after so many triumphs, Moses Kiptanui watches football on television, not athletics. Money really does talk. The same applies to many of the Brazilian footballers. My research in the Brazilian football Gold Mine killed off once and for all the illusion of Brazilian boys dashing about on the beach at Copacabana with big smiles all over their faces. The truth is that the game is deadly serious. The appetite to do what it takes has been generated by the quest for social prestige, the promise of a bulging bank account and the feeling that they have an obligation to help their families out of poverty. It's pure cash flow motivation. Thiago Mendez, director of the successful football academy Sendas Pão de Açúcar, told me: 'If you give him 100 euros you can get a young Brazilian footballer to do anything you want.'

This is not the same as saying that Moses Kiptanui and the Brazilian footballers don't love what they do. Inner passion does have a role to play, no doubt about it. I just do not believe that if we simply examine our hearts, the right path will reveal itself. This is one of the biggest misconceptions about motivation.

The traditional idea that an intrinsic source of passion fuels perseverance means that first you have to find out what you really burn for within. Apparently, once you have done that, self-discipline and persistence should emerge as a by-product. But while it is certainly true that extremely persistent people are usually passionate about what they do, this does not necessarily mean that the passion came first. As Angela Duckworth has emphasised in her studies of grit, perseverance can itself foster passion. It's often the case that the most fascinating depths and nuances of the subject do not open themselves to us until we have really absorbed ourselves in our work and dedicated ourselves to the extent that we, as Duckworth says, 'understand it and are enlivened by it'. In other words: first you must *decide* to persevere, and then passion will grow. Or as Moses Kiptanui puts it: 'You learn to love what you do.'

For instance, in a study of 24 pianists, all of whom had been finalists in at least one significant international competition, psychologist Benjamin Bloom concluded that they had all been forced to pick up their instrument and practise early in their careers. None of them had spontaneously walked over to a piano and started playing. This does not mean that they had no passion. You will never become one of the world's elite in your field without that, but their passion only fully emerged after they had been playing it for some time. They were deeply dependent on extrinsic factors to grow that passion.

My research in the Gold Mines showed that the passion

it takes to become world class is not something that comes tumbling out of the sky. You have to work for it.

Train, sleep, eat ... and do it again

Another mistake when it comes to motivation is the way that we frequently measure and judge it purely on the basis of how much effort a person puts in and how hard they work. We assume that if someone is really busy that they must be super-motivated. Hard work is certainly a good indicator of motivation, but it is not the whole story by any means. Having real drive is about much more than that. It also depends a great deal on what we do when we are not working; how we structure our lives around that long, hard slog. This occurred to me for the first time when I was in Iten, where I met one of the world's best 1,500 metres runners, Augustine Choge, who broke the long-standing 4×1,500 metres relay world record with a Kenyan team in September 2009.

I watch him train, forcing his body to endure a succession of merciless interval runs. Afterwards we get into his big white Land Rover – the only outward sign of his success – and his drives me to his home. I'm a little nonplussed when we turn in to a grass field in front of two dilapidated shacks.

'Is this where you live?' I ask him.

He nods. By Western standards it looks more like a shed than a place anybody would want to live – and certainly not the world's fastest 1,500 metres runner. The rusty hinges squeak as he opens the crooked wooden door and shows me in to his living room. There isn't much in the way of furniture – an old massage couch and a sofa full of holes.

An antiquated television set is chattering away on a table. The walls are papered with old newspapers. Behind the tiny living room is an even tinier double room with a bunk bed. This is where Augustine sleeps. But not alone, it transpires; he shares his accommodation with David Rudisha, the 800 metres world record holder.

I find it hard to believe what I see as I sit in the living room while Augustine boils water on his little gas cooker to make the Kenyan tea he drinks after every training session. This man has made good money from his sport. He could easily buy himself a fashionable flat in Nairobi. Nevertheless, he isolates himself in this little chicken shack in Iten all year round – apart from the few months when he is competing in Europe. These are, as he tells me, the optimum conditions for doing what it takes: sleep, train, eat, sleep, train, eat, again and again.

Such modest conditions are familiar to practically all Kenya's top runners, who pursue a simple lifestyle during their preparations for major competitions. I hear on several occasions during my time in Iten how world-class athletes – who have already earned millions from their sport – leave their families for months at a time to isolate themselves under austere conditions prior to major events.

A world devoid of distractions

This is in stark contrast to the average Western lifestyle, where everything feels rushed. We celebrate fast reactions rather than considered reflection. We have to-do lists, smart phones, pop-up reminders on our computers and we are constantly sending and receiving emails and text messages. Starved of time we take pride in multitasking. Work never ends. This means that many people survive on far too little sleep – on average, children worldwide get one hour less sleep than they did 30 years ago. We lack focus and purpose, and feel constantly on the brink of burning out. As world-renowned performance psychologist Dr Jim Loehr explains, we find ourselves in a constant imbalance between expenditure of energy and renewal of that energy. This can have dramatic performance consequences – anything from a loss of passion, to increased likelihood of injury, to full-scale nervous breakdown. In their book *The Power of Full Engagement*, Jim Loehr and Tony Schwartz describe how energy, not time, is the fundamental currency of high performance. The number of hours is fixed, but the quantity and quality of energy available to us is not. The more responsibility we take for the energy we bring to a task, the more powerful and productive we become.

Let us return for a moment to Anders Ericsson's ground-breaking studies of the violinists at the music academy in Berlin.

Apart from the fact that the best of them had practised much more than the next best, Ericsson discovered another crucial difference which distinguished the best violinists. They slept more. Not just at night; they also took a siesta after lunch. 'The argument they gave,' says Ericsson, 'was that the real constraint on how much you could practise was not the number of hours in the day, but the number of hours in the day you could sustain full concentration. If you couldn't sustain your concentration, you were wasting your time.' The many hours they spent training were so mentally taxing that they needed to spend a lot of time revitalising themselves.

This brings us back to the point: motivation is not just

a question of working harder at an ever-increasing rate. It is also about proper balance; deliberately investing time in energy renewal. You must not only train like a champ, you must sleep like one.

As triple steeplechase world champion Moses Kiptanui told me: 'Recovery is as important as training. But not recovery in the sense most people understand it. If your brain is working while you are recovering, it means that you're actually not recovering at all. Quality recovery *is* training.'

And Colm O'Connell was keen to stress: 'Many people talk about training, but I speak to my athletes just as much about recovery.'

During my stay in Iten I frequently spoke to European runners and I kept hearing how they improved their standard every time they visited. Not because they trained harder or differently, but because they adopted the Kenyan life-style. Train, sleep and eat – nothing else! From the age of thirteen, Kenyans and Ethiopians live and train in a way that Westerners do only when they are on an intensive training camp. As the former half-marathon world champion Lornah Kiplagat says: 'During the periods when I train hardest, I spend sixteen hours a day in bed. It is difficult to adopt this kind of lifestyle in the West, where there are far more distractions and stress factors. Mobile phones, television, and the internet are only a few of the things that can disrupt your focus. The ability to recover is underestimated as one of the explanations of the East Africans' success. Our lifestyle facilitates quality recovery to a much higher degree.'

It's actually pretty simple. Increase the demands you are making on yourself and it becomes necessary to recover your energy more effectively. Fail to do so and performance levels will fall dramatically. However, the problem is that in many environments, particularly businesses, the need for recovery is often seen as weakness, rather than an important prerequisite for sustained performance. Jim Loehr points out that: 'We give almost no attention to renewing or expanding our energy individually or organisationally.'

Anybody who wants to make a major impact on their performance must, like the East African runners, understand that motivation is not just about doing more and pushing harder. It's also about building routines for how to manage our energy more efficiently and intelligently. Otherwise we simply become flat-liners.

Man's search for meaning

Any discussion of motivation is simultaneously completely universal and enormously personal. Universal, because ambition and passion are a must if you want to improve your performance, regardless of who you are and where you come from. Personal, because what creates and maintains ambition and passion for one person may not be what does for another. Because of this it is dangerous to start talking of the right or wrong motivation.

In 1946 the Austrian neurologist and psychiatrist Viktor Frankl published his book *Man's Search for Meaning*, which has been hailed as one of the ten most influential books ever written. Frankl spent three years in concentration camps during World War II, including Theresienstadt, Auschwitz and Dachau. It was during this period that he formulated many of his key ideas. His book gives a firsthand account of his experiences during the Holocaust, and describes the psychotherapeutic method he pioneered, Logotherapy, which is founded on the belief that *striving to find meaning in life* is the most powerful motivation for human beings. Frankl's mother, father, brother and pregnant wife perished in the concentration camps. He lost everything that could be taken from a person, apart from one thing: 'the last of the human freedoms, to choose one's attitude in any given set of circumstances, to choose one's own way'. Frankl describes how some of the prisoners at Auschwitz were able to find meaning in their lives, for example by helping each other through the day. Small meaningful moments gave them the strength and the will to endure.

Frankl himself found meaning by helping his fellow prisoners hold on to their psychological health. As he writes: 'We had to learn for ourselves, and furthermore we had to teach the despairing men, that it did not matter what we expected from life, but rather what life expected from us. We needed to stop asking about the meaning of life but instead to think of ourselves as those who were being questioned by life, daily and hourly.'

Frankl's ideas have since been taken up and built on by scientists the world over. Many of them have attempted, for example, to test the importance of meaning in the business world, and the results are crystal clear: people are willing to perform the most menial of tasks, even for low pay, as long as they consider the work to be meaningful or are recognised for their contribution.

In his study 'Man's search for meaning: the case of Legos', Duke University Professor Dan Ariely set out to understand how 'perceived meaning' affects a person's motivation and willingness to work. Ariely asked two groups of people to build Lego models. The Lego models built by one group of participants were left on the table in front of them so that they could enjoy the results of their work and the supervisor would give them a new box of Lego bricks to build more toys. Hence, as the session progressed, the completed Lego toys would accumulate on the desk. The work they did had enduring results which gave the task meaning.

By contrast, each model made by the other group was removed from the table as soon as it was completed. The supervisor would then take the models apart and put the bricks back into the box. The models made by this group were not allowed to accumulate; members of the group were constantly reusing the same bricks. Their work had no enduring results and so in a sense their task was meaningless.

There was no other difference between the conditions of the two groups.

Surprisingly, the average number of models a person was willing to build significantly differed between the two groups. Although the physical requirements of the task were identical for the two groups, the subjects whose models were preserved built 30 per cent more Lego toys than those in the setup in which the meaning of their work had been taken away.

As Ariely concluded: 'These experiments clearly demonstrate what many of us have known intuitively for some time. Doing meaningful work is rewarding in itself, and we are willing to do more work for less pay when we feel our work has some sort of purpose, no matter how small.'

How can you possibly beat Shelly-Ann Fraser?

This constant search for significance in what we do is crucial to all of us, whether we are top athletes, managers, musicians or parents. As the American author Malcolm Gladwell writes: 'Hard work without meaning is a prison.'

The problem in the business world is that often the end-purpose of a company has been broken down into so many disparate tasks that workers feel very little connection with that end result, and as a consequence feel very little motivation. Dan Ariely advises managers to find ways in which they can add more meaning to even the simplest and most routine job functions: 'It's a question of educating employees about the goals of their work, and the way individual tasks fit into the bigger picture, as one way of overcoming perceived lack of meaning in work.'

It's important for a company to fire an enthusiasm for what it does externally as well as internally. A vital aspect of any CEO's job is communicating a company's raison d'être in such a way as to ensure that people relevant to the business feel engaged and enthused. Communicating that a company has a deeper purpose than simply making as much money as possible is vital.

Let us take Lego as an example. The company basically just makes plastic bricks, but there is far more to it than that. When children play with Lego bricks they train the right (creative) and left (logical) sides of their brain simultaneously. In other words, they are involved in systematic creativity. Thus Lego could argue that they are helping to train and inspire tomorrow's problem-solvers. Think about it: which company do you think people would prefer to go the extra mile for? One that makes plastic bricks or the one that trains tomorrow's problem-solvers? The answer is easy.

Giving a clear message about the meaning of a company also helps to attract the best possible workforce. Talent flocks to organisations that project a strong sense of purpose. The opposite is also true – capable people flee from places where their jobs feel purposeless or where their objectives do not feel genuine. If an organisation's underlying meaning is powerful enough you can be sure that people will grab the opportunity to contribute, even if their job involves challenging or monotonous tasks. The power of meaning to motivate us applies in our private lives as well. Just see what happens when people have children: they suddenly have a lifelong source of meaning for which they will fight and do anything.

It is the same for elite athletes. They must be capable of finding and sustaining a powerful sense of meaning in what they do if they are to be among the best. The key to lasting high performance in any field is to find a compelling mission, one for which you are willing to suffer a lot of lactic acid.

This brings us back to Shelly-Ann Fraser. There is no doubt that she has found meaning in what she does. And how can you beat a opponent who knows that her victories save lives in the neighbourhood where she grew up? For Shelly-Ann Fraser a race is not just a question of putting one foot in front of the other and running 100 metres as fast as possible. It involves much more than that.

The same applies to many of the Brazilian footballers. In 2009 a group of students from Nyköping in Sweden went to Brazil to study what drives the nation's footballers. They quizzed players between the ages of thirteen and nineteen at some of the biggest clubs across the country, asking why they played football. They asked the same question of players the same age in Sweden.

Almost without exception, the Brazilians replied that they played to earn money to help their families. In comparison, Swedish boys didn't mention their families. They just wanted to be famous.

It is not difficult to guess which of these motivating forces is the stronger. For Brazilians it's not just about football. It's about creating a better life for your nearest and dearest.

In Bekoji, too, people have an overwhelming sense of purpose. As Sentayehu Eshetu, a self-made coach explained to me: 'If you want to understand the secret of Bekoji, you must understand that kids here have nothing. They are willing to do anything to succeed.'

The West is spoiled by choice. You want to be a film-maker? Take a class. Got no money? Apply for a grant. In Bekoji there are no reality television shows or line-up auditions. Rural East Africans have to be thinking constantly about how they will survive; how they will carve out a life for themselves. Standing still does not pay. The surest way to succeed is to keep putting one foot in front of the other, and Ethiopians excel at this.

Hunger in paradise

When I deliver lectures on high performance to companies and organisations in the West, I often ask the audience the question: 'How can you create hunger in paradise?'

Most of us live very comfortable lives where we really don't need to put ourselves on the line to ensure our quality of life. This is not an environment that creates top performances.

When everything is going to plan and running smoothly, it is only natural to feel the flow; to feel motivated. But when the going gets tough it is important to have a hoard of good reasons to get out there and do it anyway. Are you hungry enough to maintain your momentum at times when you least feel like making the effort? This is the paradox of motivation. The greatest payback often comes when you least want to carry on, and it is almost certainly easier to convince yourself that it is worth continuing if you are running for the sake of your family than if you are only running for yourself.

A good example, which we have already mentioned in this book, is the British Lawn Tennis Association, which receives millions of pounds to develop world stars, but which consistently fails to do so. If the British LTA really wanted to produce great players, my advice would be to pull down the state-of-the art modern facilities they own and instead build public tennis courts in Brixton, one of the poorer London boroughs. If they dished out free tennis rackets and offered free qualified coaching to all interested children and young people, in ten years I promise they would get the top tennis players they have been hankering after for so long.

How to create hunger in paradise will be the billion-dollar question in years to come and I don't have the answer myself. But I do know that even the most spectacular training centre cannot beat a meaningful, burning desire to succeed.

In the end there is only one thing that counts: who wants it most?

What you should never forget about MOTIVATION

1. Nothing beats a really burning desire. It's without doubt the single most important predictor for world-class performance.

2. Why is the most powerful psychological question to boost motivation. Much more important than **what**. Any individual or organisation must ask themselves why they do what they do, and what would happen if they didn't.

3. Don't wait for the thunderbolt of passion to hit you. It's not going to happen on its own. Instead, start to act – engage and invest yourself in what you do and the passion will start to flow. Often it's perseverance that fosters passion, not the other way around.

4. Motivation is not just about doing more and pushing harder. It's also about building routines for how to manage our energy more efficiently and intelligently. It's a commitment to a lifestyle where you not only train as a champion, but also recover as a champion.

5. The form motivation that brings a person or an organisation to one goal will not necessarily bring them to their next. Often motivation has to be reignited, visions must be renewed and meaning deepened in order to to maintain momentum.

Epilogue

The journey to achieving top performance can be insanely exciting at times; and incredibly frustrating at others. Exciting because the desire to develop, discover, create, learn, achieve, change and improve – whether the activity is playing the violin, running marathons, painting pictures or leading a group of people – is one of the greatest sources of happiness and satisfaction a person can know. Frustrating because every time we reach the summit of a mountain we know there is another mountain waiting for us a bit further along the track. There is always something bigger and better out there; something new to master. The journey will never end.

In Indonesia they have a beautiful expression for travel: *to rinse your eyes*. When you stay at home, caught up in the routines of your everyday life, your vision becomes cloudy. When the same things pass before your eyes day in, day out, you stop being about to really *see* them. When you hear the same words spoken again and again, you stop really listening. Travelling gives you your eyes and ears back. It blows away the cobwebs and forces you to see the world afresh. This is precisely how it was for me when I travelled to the Gold Mines. That journey really began five years ago when I overlooked the potential possessed by Simon Kjaer. I was no longer looking or listening properly – or perhaps I was just looking and listening for the wrong signals. The realisation that I had overlooked Simon was tremendously frustrating, but it also aroused a fierce curiosity in me. That ultimately led to me selling everything I owned and setting off to travel the world for six months.

It is my profound conviction that regardless of whether you are engaged in developing high performance as an executive, a coach, a teacher, a parent, a musician or an athlete, one of the greatest dangers is in becoming locked in to a particular way of viewing the world; in becoming mired in routine. We all need to rinse our eyes.

Meeting a man like Stephen Francis sharpens your senses. You begin to see subtleties and distinctions you didn't even know existed. When you realise what the world's leading researchers have proved – that in-built talent counts for much less than hard work and commitment – you feel inspired to reach that little bit further, knowing that things that you thought were not attainable actually are. And when you hear what Colm O'Connell and the Kenyan runners have to tell you, there is a sense of relief that the recipe for high performance is perhaps not as complicated as we often believe – difficult, yes, but not complicated.

The Gold Mines reveal a future of incredible possibilities for each and every one of us.

I'm convinced that everyone, wherever they may come from, has an inner drive; a desire to live out their full potential and to make a difference in the world. And as I wrote in the introduction to this book, it is now more important than ever to bring that drive into play. No other resource will be more crucial for organisations – and society as a whole – in years to come than the ability to identify, develop and motivate talent. The unconventional methods, ideas and angles on talent development served up by the Gold Mines will hopefully challenge and inspire you to meet that challenge. The object of this book has been to rinse your eyes.

Notes

Chapter 1: The secret is not a secret

Tanser, T. *More Fire: How to Run the Kenyan Way* (Westholme Publishing, 2008).

Ash, G.I., Scott, R.A., Deason, M., Dawson, T.A., Wolde, B., Bekele, Z., Teka, S. and Pitsiladis, Y.P. 'No Association between ACE Gene Variation and Endurance Athlete Status in Ethiopians' *Medicine and Science in Sports and Exercise* (2011).

Scott, R.A. et al. 'ACTN3 and ACE genotypes in elite Jamaican and US sprinters' *Medicine and Science in Sports and Exercise* (2010).

Fudge, B.W., Easton, C., Kingsmore, D., Kiplamai, F.K., Onywera, V.O., Westerterp, K.R., Kayser, B., Noakes, T.D. and Pitsiladis, Y.P. 'Elite Kenyan endurance runners are hydrated day-to-day with ad libitum fluid intake' *Medicine and Science in Sports and Exercise* (2008).

Fudge, B.W., Westerterp, K.R., Kiplamai, F.K., Onywera, V.O., Boit, M.K., Kayser, B. and Pitsiladis, Y.P. 'Evidence of negative energy balance using doubly labelled water in elite Kenyan endurance runners prior to competition' *British Journal of Nutrition* (2006).

Saltin, B., Kim, C.K., Terrados, N., Larsen, H., Svedenhag, J. and Rolf, C.J. 'Morphology, enzyme activities and buffer capacity in leg muscles of Kenyan and Scandinavian runners' *Scandinavian Journal of Medicine and Science in Sports* (1995).

Saltin, B., Larsen, H., Terrados, N., Bangsbo, J., Bak, T., Kim, C.K., Svedenhag, J. and Rolf, C.J. 'Aerobic exercise capacity at sea level and at altitude in Kenyan boys, junior and senior runners compared with Scandinavian runners' *Scandinavian Journal of Medicine and Science in Sports* (1995).

Timmons, J.A., Knudsen, S., Rankinen, T., et al. 'Using molecular classification to predict gains in maximal aerobic capacity following endurance exercise training in humans' *J. Applied Physiology* (2010).

Rankinen, T., Roth, S.M., Bray, M.S., Loos, R.J., Peruse, L., Wolfarth, B., Hagberg, J.M. and Bouchard, C. 'Advances in exercise, fitness, and performance genomics' *Medical Science Sports Exercise* (2010).

Bouchard, C. 'Genomic predictors of trainability' *Experimental Physiology* (2011).

Flynn, J.R. *What is Intelligence?* (Cambridge University Press, 2007).

Flynn, J.R. *Asian Americans – Achievement Beyond IQ* (Routledge, 1991).

Dawkins, R. *The Selfish Gene* (Oxford University Press, 1976).

Doll, J. and Mayr, U. *Intelligence and Achievement in Chess – A Study of Chess Masters* (Psychologische Beitrage, 1997).

Hudsom, L. *Contrary Imaginations – A Psychological Study of the English Schoolboy* (Penguin, 1967).

Chapter 2: What you see is not what you get

Anders, G. *The Rare Find – Spotting Exceptional Talent Before Everyone Else* (Penguin, 2011).

Helsen, W.F., Van Winckel, J. and Williams, M. *The Relative Age Effect in Youth Soccer Across Europe* (2004).

Robinson, K. *The Element – How Finding Your Passion Changes Everything* (Penguin, 2010).

Gladwell, M. *What the Dog Saw and Other Adventures* (Penguin, 2009).

Gallway, T. *The Inner Game of Work* (Random House, 1999).

Charan, R. and Conaty, B. *The Talent Masters – Why Smart Leaders Put People Before Numbers* (Random House, 2010).

Lewis, M. *Moneyball – The Art of Winning an Unfair Game* (Norton, 2004).

Duckworth, A., Quinn, P. and Tsukayama, E. 'The roles of IQ and self-control in predicting standardized achievement test scores and report card grades' *Journal of Educational Psychology* (2011).

Barnsley, R. 'The Relative Age Effect in Football' *International Review for the Sociology of Sport* (1992).

Barnsley, R. and Thompson, A.H. 'Hockey success and birth date: The relative age effect revisited' *International Review for the Sociology of Sport* (2010).

Chapter 3: Start early or die soon

Ericsson, K.A. *Cambridge Handbook of Expertise and Expert Performance* (Cambridge University Press, 2006).

Chi, M.T.H. and Ceci, S.J. 'Content knowledge: it's role, representation, and restructuring in memory development' *Advances in Child Development* (1987).

Ericsson, K.A. 'Exceptional memorizers: made, not born' *Trends in Cognitive Sciences* (2003).

Ericsson, K.A., *The influence of experience and deliberate practice on the development of superior expert performance* (Cambridge University Press, 2006).

Ericsson, K.A., Charness, N. 'Expert performance: its structure and acquisition' *American Psychologist* (1994).

Ericsson, K.A. 'Attaining excellence through deliberate practice: insights from the study of expert performance' *The Pursuit of Excellence in Education* (1994).

Ericsson, K.A. 'Deliberate practice and the acquisition and maintenance of expert performance in medicine and related domains' *Academic Medicine* (2004).

Lehmann, A.C. and Ericsson, K.A. *The historical development of domains of expertise: performance standards and innovations in music* (Oxford University Press, 1994).

Sloboda, J.A., Davidson, J.W., Michael, J., Howe, A. and Moore, D.G. 'The role of practice in development of performing musicians' *British Journal of Psychology* (1996).

De Groot, A.D. *Thought and Choice in Chess* (Mouton, 1946).

Levitin, D.J. *This is Your Brain on Music: Understanding a Human Obsession* (Dutton, 2006).

Howe, M.J.A. *Genius Explained* (Cambridge University Press, 1999).

Morris, J.M. *Mozart as a Working Stiff* (Cambridge University Press, 1994).

Woods, E. and McDaniel, P. *Training a Tiger: a Father's Guide to Raising a Winner in Both Golf and Life* (HarperCollins, 1997).

Howe, M.J.A. *The Psychology of Human Learning* (1980), *The Early Lives of Child Prodigies* (1993), *Gifts, Talents and Natural Abilities: an Explanatory Mythology* (1990).

Klawans, H.L. *Why Michael Couldn't Hit* (W.H. Freeman, 1996).

Rooney, W. *My Story So Far* (HarperSport, 2006).

Iyengar, S. 'How much choice is too much? Determinants of individual contributions' *Pension Design and Structure: New Lessons from Behavioral Finance* (2004).

Iyengar, S. and DeVoe, S. *Rethinking the Value of Choice: Considering Cultural Mediators of Intrinsic Motivation In Cross-Cultural Differences in Perspectives on the Self* (Lawrence Erlbaum Associates, 2003).

Iyengar, S. and Lepper, M.R. 'Choice and its consequences: on the costs and benefits of self-determination in self and motivation' *Emerging Psychological Perspectives* (2002).

Loehr, J., Schwartz, T. *The Power of Full Engagement* (Simon & Schuster, 2004).

Chapter 4: We're all quitters

Onywera, V.O., Scott, R.A., Boit, M.K. and Pitsiladis, Y. Kenyan Endurance Runners *Journal of Sports Sciences* (2006).

Christensen, D.L. *Washindi – Runners from Kalendjin* (Frydenlund Publishing, 2000).

Tanser, T. *More Fire: How to Run the Kenyan Way* (Westholme Publishing, 2008).

Klopfer, B. Psychological Variables in Human Cancer *Journal of Projective Techniques* (1957).

Syed, M. *Bounce – How Champions are Made* (Fourth Estate, 2011).

Isaac, A. R. 'Mental practice – does it work in the field?' *The Sport Psychologist* (1992).

Martin, K.A. and Hall, C.R. 'Using mental imagery to enhance intrinsic motivation' *Journal of Sport and Exercise Psychology* (1995).

Murphy, S. 'Models of imagery in sport psychology' *Journal of Mental Imagery* (1990).

Orlick, T., Zitzelsberger, L., Li-Wei, Z. and Qi-wei, M. 'The effect of mental-imagery training on performance enhancement with 7–10-year-old children' *The Sports Psychologist* (1992).

Pavio, A. 'Cognitive and Motivational Functions of Imagery in Human Performance' *Journal of Applied Sports Science* (1982).

Pascual-Leone A. 'The Brain that Plays Music and is Changed by It' *The Cognitive Neuroscience of Music* (2003).

Noakes, T. *Lore of Running* (Human Kinetics Europe Ltd, 2002).

Samuele M., Marcora, W.S. and Manning, V. 'Mental fatigue impairs physical performance in humans' *Applied Physiology* (2009).

Amann, M., Hopkins, W.G. and Marcora, S.M. 'Similar sensitivity of time to exhaustion and time-trial time to changes in endurance' *Medical Science Sports Exercise* (2008).

Marcora, S.M., Bosio, A. and de Morree, H.M. 'Locomotor muscle fatigue increases cardiorespiratory responses and reduces performance during intense cycling exercise independently from metabolic stress' *Journal of Applied Physiology* (2008).

Chapter 5: Success is about mindset, not facilities

Steerbberg, R.J. *How Practical and Creative Intelligence Determine Success in Life* (Plume, 1997).

Ericsson, K. A., Whyte, J. and Ward, P. 'Expert performance in nursing:

Reviewing research on expertise in nursing within the framework of the expert-performance approach' *Advances in Nursing Science* (2007).

Ericsson, K.A. 'An expert-performance perspective on medical expertise: Study superior clinical performance rather than experienced clinicians' *Medical Education* (2007).

Bond, W., Kuhn, G., Binstadt E., Quirk, M., Wu, T., Tews, M., Dev, P. and Ericsson, K.A. 'The use of simulation in the development of individual cognitive expertise in emergency medicine' *Academic Emergency Medicine* (2008).

Ericsson, K.A. 'Deliberate practice and acquisition of expert performance: a general overview' *Academic Emergency Medicine* (2008).

Krampe, R.T. and Ericsson, K.A. 'Maintaining excellence: Deliberate practice and elite performance in young and older pianists' *Journal of Experimental Psychology* (2006).

Choudhry, N.K., Fletcher, R.H. and Soumerai, S.B. 'Systematic review: the relationship between clinical experience and quality of healthcare' *Annals of Internal Medicine* (2005).

Camerer, C.F. and Johnson, E.J. *How Can Experts Know So Much and Predict So Badly?* (The Process-performance In Expert Judgement, 1991).

Ericsson, K.A., Smith, J. *Toward a General Theory of Expertise: Prospects and Limits* (Cambridge University Press, 1991).

Holm, S. *Hojdhoppare* (Wahlström & Widstrand, 2005)

Csikszentmihalyis, M. *Flow – The Psychology of Optimal Experience* (HarperCollins, 2008).

Restak, R. *The New Brain: How the Modern Age is Rewiring Your Mind* (Rodale, 2003).

Goldsmith, M. *What Got You There Won't Get You There* (Hyperion, 2007).

Dweck, C. *Mindset – The New Psychology of Success* (Random House, 2006).

Collins, J. *How The Mighty Fall – And Why Some Companies Never Give In* (Random House, 2009).

Kotter, J.P. *A Sense of Urgency* (Harvard Business School Publishing, 2008).

Conant, D.R. and Norgaard, M. *Touchpoints – Creating Powerful Leadership Connections in the Smallest of Moments* (John Wiley & Sons, 2011).

Sengupta, K., Abdel-Hamid, T.K. and Van Wassenhove, L.N. *The Experience Trap* (Harvard Business Review, 2008).

Pink, D. *Drive – The Surprising Truth about What Motivates Us* (Canongate Books, 2010).

Chapter 6: Godfathers
Robinson, K. *The Element – How Finding Your Passion Changes Everything* (Penguins, 2010).

Chapter 7: Not pushing your kids is irresponsible

Bloom, B.S. *Developing Talent in Young People* (Ballantine Books, 1985).

Winner, E. and Gardner, H. 'Fact, fiction, and fantasy in childhood' *New Directions for Child Development* (1979).

Chapter 8: The hunger factor

Winner, E. *The Rage to Master – the Decisive Role of Talent in the Visual Arts* (Lawrence Erlbaum Associates, 1996).

Duckworth, A.L. 'The significance of self-control' *The National Academy of Sciences* (2011).

Duckworth, A., Kirby, T., Tsukayama, E., Berstein, H. and Ericsson, K. 'Deliberate practice spells success: why grittier competitors triumph at the National Spelling Bee' *Social Psychological and Personality Science* (2011).

Duckworth, A.L. and Quinn, P.D. 'Development and validation of the Short Grit Scale (Grit-S)' *Journal of Personality Assessment* (2009).

Duckworth, A.L., Peterson, C., Matthews, M.D. and Kelly, D.R. 'Grit: perseverance and passion for long-term goals' *Journal of Personality and Social Psychology* (2007).

Duckworth, A.L. and Seligman, M.E.P. 'Self-discipline outdoes IQ in predicting academic performance of adolescents' *Psychological Science* (2005).

Duckworth, A.L., Steen, T.A. and Seligman, M.E.P. 'Positive psychology in clinical practice' *Annual Review of Clinical Psychology* (2005).

Winner, E. *Gifted children: myths and realities* (BasicBooks, 1997).

Terman, L. *The Measurement of Intelligence* (1916), *The Use of Intelligence Tests* (1916), *Genetic Studies of Genius* (Houghton Mifflin, 1925, 1947, 1959).

Renzulli, J.S. *What Makes Giftedness? Re-examining a Definition* (Phi Delta Kappa, 1978).

Renzulli, J.S. *Schools for talent development: A practical plan for total school improvement* (Creative Learning Press, 1994).

Walton, G. and Cohens, G. 'Mere Belonging' *Journal of Personality and Social Psychology* (2007).

Frankl, V.E. *Man's Search for Meaning* (Simon & Schuster, 1997).

Ariely, D., Kamenica, E. and Prelec, D. 'Man's search for meaning: the case of Legos' *Journal of Economic Behavior and Organization* (2008).

Index